UNLEASHING GREATNESS

PATHWAY 1 FOUNDATION
INSPIRING A LEGACY OF COURAGE

This book was written to share Pathway 1 and to generate revenue for the Pathway 1 Foundation. The foundation will provide scholarships for: (1) young New Zealanders striving to 'Unleash their Greatness' on the world stage (e.g. in sport, music, the arts or academia) and who do not have the financial support to 'fly'; and (2) research into how to deal with the plastic waste that is destroying our oceans.

As part of living to our foundation's vision, 'inspiring a legacy of courage', we challenge you to read the book then pass it on to someone who you think will benefit from it but may not be able to afford a copy themselves; thereby inspiring them to unleash their greatness. Simply put your name below, date it and put in a message. Then when that person has finished with the book they can do the same thing, and ignite the Pathway 1 legacy!

If you would like to contribute to the Pathway 1 Foundation please feel free to contact the author on **mopuniverse@gmail.com**

NAME	DATE	MESSAGE

UNLEASHING GREATNESS

DAVID GALBRAITH

In Sport and Life Through the Pathway of Courage

This book is dedicated to you. It is your time to fly.
LIVE PURE!

CONTENTS

Foreword by Stephen Donald	7
Introduction	9
Pathway 1: The Pathway of Courage	13
Pathway 1 and the Impossible Dream	49
Committing Fully to the Dream	65
Developing the Strategic Plan to Success	105
Building Powerful Non-outcome Success Rules	129
Moments of Perfection: MOP Universe!	169
The Goose Bump Moment	195
Training-to-Win and the Importance of Deep Practice	225
The Honey Badger Mind Week	243
Final Mind Warrant of Fitness Check	269
Afterword	279
Appendix 1	281
Acknowledgements	285
About the Author	286
Image Credits	287

Author's Note

I have been incredibly privileged to meet so many world-class people during my years as a performance psychologist, none more inspirational than Stephen Donald. He is a generous character, whose absolute love of, and loyalty to, his teammates makes him worth his weight in gold. He is also a very handy rugby player. The photo below is from the 2011 Rugby World Cup final. I like it because it shows he had a great game that day, even though he will be most remembered for the kick that won the game (and his poor-fitting jersey). It is an absolute honour to have him write the foreword for this book.

Cheers 'Beaver'.

New Zealand All Blacks World Cup-winning first five, Stephen Donald.

FOREWORD

Before meeting DG, I had always thought sports psychology was not for your common New Zealand man such as myself. It certainly was not a topic that I would bring up over a few beers with my mates; it was a sign of weakness, it was simply not cool. Then, a few years back, before the start of another Super Rugby campaign with the Chiefs, my team and I were introduced to the new 'head doctor'. I sat back in my chair at Waikato Stadium, wondering how I was going to amuse myself for the next few hours. I concluded that I would watch the phenomenon that was Siti (my teammate) sleeping with his eyes open.

However, before I got a chance to drift off, he was teaching us how to talk to beautiful women at a bar. I was listening! The guts of it, he told us, was that you have to believe in what you've got and be confident with it. I would later learn that this is what DG calls Pathway 1.

David's Pathway 1 is a simple approach to the 'often mysterious' world of sports psychology. For a simple man like myself, Pathway 1 was ideal. It's simply a question that challenges you to ask yourself, **'Is my current action from courage and going to be beneficial to my efforts in getting where I want to be as a rugby player?'**

However, as a professional sportsman, you have a lot of

downtime when your mind can play tricks on you. The mind starts to take notice of the bad things about you in the press, you miss a kick you shouldn't have, and suddenly Pathway 1 is a tough track to follow.

David has a great concept for how his athletes can get back to Pathway 1 when things get tough. We came up with our own positive-aggressive phrases to clear the mind and get back on track. Mine was a very simple and powerful two-word phrase!

In 2010, after a chest operation, I immersed myself in Pathway 1 to the point that I was falling asleep kicking goals, and by the time I came back for Waikato I was in a great head space, which led to six weeks of probably the best form of my career. At the end of 2010, however, after working my way back to the All Blacks, an unfortunate event occurred during a test match in Hong Kong that really knocked my confidence, and put me on a bit of a detour from living Pathway 1.

It was about a 10-month detour, during which time things were pretty tough confidence-wise, but looking back now, those events certainly helped me strengthen my commitment to living and playing from Pathway 1. By the time October 2011 came around, the Rugby World Cup final at Eden Park, everything that had happened and been said about me as a rugby player since Hong Kong was met with my little two-word phrase, and I was back on Pathway 1.

What makes David's approach so easy to follow for an athlete is that it's all about positive intent, and when you are under pressure, such as in a World Cup final, and you have to perform, the only way to be successful is by being positive with huge intent. Come to think of it, life is no different!

I hope you get as much from this tall, skinny white guy as I did.

All the best!
Beaver [Stephen Donald]

INTRODUCTION

There is a secret to success: **courage**! The courage to dream big. Then the courage to ignore all those people who tell you that what you seek is impossible, even your own negative, limiting internal thoughts and beliefs. The courage, in fact, to tell them all to get stuffed! The courage to approach the key people you will need to help you along the way. The courage to plan and act repeatedly, often for many, many years. The courage to accept that this may be the only thing you ever have the time to really commit to in your entire life. Then the courage to say 'NO', so that nothing comes between you and your vision. The courage to be honest with yourself about whether you are truly 'paying the price' required or 'just doing enough' and going through the motions. The courage to deal with repeated setbacks and failings, then wake up the next morning and get back to work. The courage to have the patience and discipline to keep doing what works, no matter how small and seemingly insignificant it may be. Then the courage to remain humble and not get complacent or comfortable when you start to succeed along the way. This book is about how to grow and master the level of courage needed to do these things.

What proof do I have that the material covered in this book works? Firstly, it worked for me. It gave me a way to unleash my mind and potential at a crossroads in my life that led to here and, without courage, would have led to psychiatric inpatient care, of that I am certain.

At 29 years old, my life was paralysed by powerful panic attacks bordering on psychosis; ironically while I was training as a clinical psychologist! I realised that unless I mastered courage I was doomed. I identified that the cause of my panic was that I was afraid of being beaten up and of upsetting people. So I did two things; well, three actually. First, I said to myself, 'I am sick and tired of living my life this way!' Second, I went to martial arts. And third, I set myself challenges to learn how to be courageous in places that previously had caused me fear and panic, where I was afraid of upsetting people or being judged. I forced myself to turn and face the 'dragon', and not run away from it!

For example, I drove my 1972 Holden Kingswood station wagon on the expressway all the way from Mercer to Auckland (60 kilometres) every day in the fast lane at 35 miles per hour. When people pulled up behind me and tooted their horns in annoyance, I would simply carry on driving slowly. They would eventually pass me on the inside, and often give me abuse as they drove past. I would simply smile and wave. I always had my passenger's window down as well, so I could chat to them as they drove past. Many wanted to stay for a lengthy chat!

I would do more spontaneous things as well. I gave a public speech in the Pukekohe town square about child abuse and its connection to our growing littering and garbage problem. (I was working at a community agency treating sexual offenders at the time.) I stood there with two plastic milk bottles in my hands while shouting out my speech. Believe me, people walked past with very strange looks on their faces. I finished my speech, got down from my speaking area and quickly walked back to my truck. I was shaking like a leaf!

Essentially, I would use any opportunity to express myself in public in a way that would have previously caused major panic or made me negatively self-conscious. One day I drove past a public protest about protecting the Waikato River. I raced home and made up a banner that said: 'Blood on Your Children's Hands', implying that if we did not protect the river, it would be our children who suffered. I went back to the protest and started chanting my slogan. Again, many people gave me a wide berth, and looked at me like I was insane.

All the time during these challenges, I was experiencing great panic. I just kept telling myself, 'I will not be a coward. I will learn not to care what others think of me. I don't care what they think. I will express myself!' What amazed me was that, after a very short time, I felt more free than at any other time in my life. The fear of upsetting people or being judged just faded away. I was emotionally pure! It was then that my life took off.

Looking back, had I not mastered the ability to **act from courage**, my life would not have changed, and eventually it would have worn me down. I would have ended up in psychiatric care! I have been more 'successful' than I could have possibly dreamed, despite so many limiting odds. For example, I am very ugly and hairy, but despite that, I have a hot wife! All my success is because of one thing: acting from courage – staring the risk of failing and chance of success right in the face and forcing myself to unleash and go for it anyway.

The second lot of evidence I have for the concepts and guidance within this book working is the feedback from people I have worked with. This book is full of their stories and examples. They are some of New Zealand's most successful sportsmen and sportswomen, and they all agree that the concepts covered in this book have helped them unleash their minds and perform under the greatest pressure on the international sporting-world stage.

What makes me most happy is that the material covered in this book has helped them unleash themselves and achieve richer lives. That is, after all, why I do what I do. I don't really care about their results. I know that may sound like an outrageous thing to say. Of course I am happy for them when they 'win' and perform well, but what I care most about is them as people, and that they express themselves fully from a deeply pure place. They all know that if they link in with me by text or email and tell me about a result or an outcome without telling me about their spirit underneath the performance, I will not return their message, or at times may even reply, 'I don't care!' But if they talk about *how* they performed – about their courage and how they just let go and unleashed – I will phone them for all the details! That is the real magic I seek for them, and I want them to get the message that living from pure courage is the most important thing.

I cannot wait for you to experience the way it feels when you truly live from courage, the purity that comes when you free your mind of the pollution of outcome thinking (e.g. fear of failing, and hope of success and glory), unleash and drop into instinctive mode. Only when you give your heart and soul to what you do, with no expectation of 'success' or payback, can you see just how high and far you can fly!

Kind regards
DG

PATHWAY 1: THE PATHWAY OF COURAGE

Courage is the most important emotion you need to learn to control in your life. It does not matter if you are still at school, work in one of the biggest companies in the world, are an Olympian or are a social sports person, courage is critical to you unleashing your mind and achieving your potential.

For example, if you play golf and your confidence and self-belief are low and you are standing on the tee of the hardest hole on the course, or standing over a tricky little left-to-right breaking four-foot putt for par, you need courage. If you are sitting your final school exams and you are about to walk into the test of your hardest subject that you need a good score on to get into medicine at university, you need courage.

In the early stages of pursuing your dream, whatever it is, if you have minimal, if any, evidence that you can achieve it, you need courage. You need great courage to keep acting for a long period of time, possibly years, in order to achieve any dream of significance.

Many athletes experience times when they struggle. It is then that they must have the courage to be patient and keep moving forward, to keep their foot on the accelerator, and keep trusting, investing, practising and performing – to keep the dream alive. Often, it is in these times that many throw it all away. Yet, those that hang on and have the courage to push through the hard times can end up succeeding beyond their deepest expectations.

The easiest way to explain Pathway 1 is to give you a real-life example. Sir Edmund Hillary is perhaps New Zealand's most loved hero. When Hillary committed to climbing Mt Everest, it was considered physically impossible for humans to successfully reach the summit. Scientists globally believed that if you climbed above 28,000 feet you would die. At that time, Everest was thought to be 29,028 feet high. Despite knowing this information, Ed maintained his decision to attempt the climb. That conviction would have required massive courage. This was pure Pathway 1. I imagine Ed would have said something like, 'I guess we will find out then, won't we?' **It is the best life example of Pathway 1 I have ever found!**

Imagine every scientist telling you that what you are planning will result in your death; the fact Sir Ed carried on to plan and prepare to climb the mountain is quite extraordinary. His challenge of the global scientific belief is perhaps more inspiring than his actual success of climbing the mountain. Well before he and Tenzing reached the summit, he had already climbed the greatest mountain of all – the mountain within himself!

Think about that for a minute, imagine how you would feel if every scientist in the world told you an action you were about to take would kill you. Most people would be petrified. Ed had to overcome the fear of death, not merely the fear of making a mistake, or being judged, or failing and being embarrassed! He could only have planned and acted in the way he did by reaching a point at which he accepted that he could die and placed more importance on living life on his terms.

Here is what I believe Sir Ed's Pathway 1 philosophy of courage would have been:

I WOULD RATHER DIE LIVING FROM COURAGE THAN TO LIVE FROM FEAR AND DOUBT AND SPEND THE REST OF MY LIFE WONDERING WHAT I COULD HAVE ACHIEVED!

It is certainly what I would have expected Ed to have said to himself as he stood in front of the Hillary Step, a seemingly impassable 40 feet of sheer ice between him and Tenzing and the Everest summit. Lisa Carrington is the current 200-metre sprint canoe Olympic and back-to-back world champion. She has a very similar philosophy to Sir Edmund Hillary and it seems appropriate to share hers here. I think Ed would have liked it.

I WILL CHOOSE TO LIVE WHEN OTHERS CHOOSE TO CURL UP AND DIE

My philosophy of courage is choosing to live when there is also the option to 'die'. Choosing to live for me is about feeling and embracing every moment of the day, a race, training, etc. It's having the courage to be in the moment even when my stomach and mind are telling me this is too hard. When I think about picking between to live or to die, to die would go against my personal philosophy, and if I were to die I would be disappointed so I choose to live. I accept I may fail, but I also accept that there could be a great reward.

I have talked about this a lot with DG, and we related it to a lioness. A lioness needs to hunt for survival, and every time she targets her prey she knows that if she doesn't catch the antelope she and her family will die. She knows that although she may sometimes miss the kill, she will keep trying because she also knows she will make the kill, eventually!

Lisa Carrington

Every day we are presented with many moments when we make the decision to act either from courage (Pathway 1) or self-doubt from fear of failure or judgement (Pathway 2): from a discussion at work with colleagues in which you have differing views, to approaching someone you have wanted to ask for a long time to be a mentor, to hitting a driver down the out of bounds (OB) line on the hardest par five on your golf course. Even in parenting this is the case: you decide whether you have the courage to break free from the chains of traditional 'adult expectations' that can make you a grumpy policeman and become a free, loving, fun parent (e.g. one who leaves the house messy so you can play with your children at the park even though your mind screams at you that they should be at home cleaning their rooms and you should be vacuuming the house). In every one of these situations, you can decide to act from courage and do the right thing, taking the hard road, or act from cowardice and take the easy road or easy way out.

Pathway 1 is taking the hard road, and taking the action that requires the greatest courage, despite risk of failing, judgement, rejection or upsetting others, and despite fears and doubts. It is also taking the hard road in the face of potential success. Most people unfortunately choose the easy road in the face of such challenges and give in to fear and doubt. Often the mind can be very sneaky and will try to trick you into believing that you are being courageous and doing the right thing, when actually you are not. So how do you know if you are living from courage or from fear and doubt?

One of the best ways to know if you are following Pathway 1 (e.g. when you are parenting, playing sports, studying for an exam or preparing for a job interview) is to ask yourself if you are uncomfortable. Pathway 1 is characterised by being uncomfortable. This discomfort will be a result of living and playing on the edge of your potential, on the edge of failing, staring risk of failure and success right in the face and then acting despite it! Making a difficult phone call, changing your course of study, speaking up when you disagree with what others are saying, or hitting a strong putt when the club championships are on the line, despite being petrified of three-putting, are all wonderful examples of choosing to live by Pathway 1, the pathway of courage.

Living pure Pathway 1 is incredibly challenging however, as is reflected in the following quote by one of New Zealand's best golf coaches, Jay Carter. Jay is the appointed golf coach to the New Zealand Eisenhower team and other New Zealand golf squads, and is based at the Tauranga Golf Club.

MY REALISATION I WAS NOT LIVING PATHWAY 1

I think I have spent my whole life living in Pathway 2. Over the last few years, since meeting David, I thought I was edging closer to Pathway 1, but I think all that happened was I became aware of the two pathways and convinced myself I was living Pathway 1, when all I was doing was living in 'bullsh*t world', a world filled with excuses and reassurance, in which I was too afraid to make a decision without seeking affirmation from those around me that everything would be okay.

For me the big turning point was the simple realisation that I was actually the one in control of what was happening to my life around me and I had to make a conscious decision to take action, the one thing I have avoided my whole life. It was one simple line in an email from David that made everything click into place: '. . . that stops from tonight!' That one sentence made me take action; there was no more waiting for the right time, starting next Monday or next month, it was stopping tonight!

When I thought about what that meant, I realised that this was what living Pathway 1 was all about. In the past I knew what Pathway 1 was, but I didn't know what living it looked like or felt like, because I had convinced myself I was already there. But the reality was I was in bullsh*t world, which is a far cry from Pathway 1.

Jay working with Mark Brown at the Tauranga Golf Club in New Zealand.

Once I had this breakthrough, things started to change. Previous issues that I would shy away from I tackled head on and enjoyed the challenge. I seemed to seek reassurance no longer and instead made decisions that I knew were right even if they were hard, and as a result the need for reassurance subsided. I have reread that email every day since, and it continues to challenge me. I am by no means fully living Pathway 1 yet, but I am certainly not in bullsh*t world either, and I am not spending my time waiting for the right moment and letting things pass me by.

Jay Carter

PATHWAY 1: EXERCISE 1

Self-Reflection: Are You Living from Pathway 1 Courage?

To find out whether you are living from Pathway 1 or not, simply ask yourself:

Am I 'careful' in life?

Am I careful not to upset others, careful not to get things wrong at school, careful not to go out of bounds or to three-putt when I play golf, careful not to be rejected by others, careful not to lose my hard-earned money?

If you are careful, then you are not Pathway 1. If you are careful, you are living from self-doubt and fear of bad outcomes (e.g. failing) or what I call 'living from Pathway 2'. Ironically you are not living at all, you are just dying slowly!

Now ask yourself this question and write your answers below:

How much has being careful cost me?

For example, being careful may have cost you many opportunities to push your potential as a golfer and to go for it (e.g. not going to the big city to work and play under a world-class coach). Being careful may have cost you an opportunity to go to university and study medicine as you settled for a sport and recreation course instead. Being careful may have cost you an opportunity to marry the woman or man of your dreams as you settled for second best because deep down you thought you were not good enough for 'the one' . . .

List here what being careful has cost you:

_____

_____

_____

_____

_____

_____

Hopefully doing this exercise will have annoyed you a lot! Write a few short notes to yourself here. Be strong in what you say to yourself about what you need to stop doing and what you need to change – no one else will read it!

_____

_____

_____

_____

_____

Now let's use that annoyance to fuel a Pathway 1 change. If you found that you are not living Pathway 1, tell yourself the following statements:

I am sick and tired of living my life this way!

I am sick and tired of being careful or being afraid!

I will not accept living like this any more!

Living this way stops right now!

Notice how saying these things makes you feel. It should inject solid determination to change. It was the key to me turning my life around at

29, and I have repeatedly seen it as a critical step in others moving to live from courage and starting to live fully. We actually have to decide to change before anything actually does!

Now list three actions you will take **immediately** (not later, not tomorrow - NOW) that will drive your life into Pathway 1 (e.g. phone the woman or man of your dreams and ask her or him out for a coffee; change your university study online to the subjects you really want to take; book a lesson to learn how to draw the golf ball). Do not carry on with this exercise or continue reading this book until you have completed these three things. Go and do them now!

1. _____

_____

_____

2. _____

_____

_____

3. _____

_____

_____

Well done! Notice how you feel. More than likely you feel proud, excited, scared and uncomfortable, all at the same time. That is how you will know you are living Pathway 1. You will feel these emotions often, but best of all, you will feel ALIVE! That is what living should feel like. Take a mental note: use this as your benchmark for every day living from now until your heart does actually stop beating! Imagine the life you will live.

Now download and print an image from the Internet that reflects what you are feeling, and put it here.

PATHWAY 1: THE PATHWAY OF COURAGE 23

Sir Ed's natural conviction to operate from Pathway 1 would have been based on a deep philosophy or attitude to live his life from courage and to push his limits as far as possible. This is evident in a great quote of his: 'Why would you set a goal you have even a small idea you can achieve?' I absolutely love this quote! It radically changed the way I thought about goal setting and made me acutely aware of how I had lived my life from the locked-in mindset that all goals needed to be 'realistic'. Not any more! Every time I catch myself setting a realistic long-term outcome goal (different from daily objectives such as 50 putts or short-term goals over a few months) I remind myself of Sir Ed's philosophy. This helps me live from the pathway of courage and it will help you live the same way.

Sir Ed's goal-setting philosophy gives us an insight into how his mind was wired. It was unacceptable to him to plan or behave in any other way than to live on the edge of his potential and see just how far he could reach and grow. Any decision he made, any goal he set, any adventure he decided on pursuing would have been based on courage and an expectation to push his limits, and in his case this often meant to the edge of life and death. I am sure that if you adopted this philosophy (and this is not saying that you have to undertake extreme life-threatening adventures) and simply applied it to your work, where you live, what you do for a hobby, who you spend time with and how you 'live' your sport, in one year from now your world would look dramatically different, and for the better. By living fully in Pathway 1, the pathway of courage, your life can look profoundly different in just one day! Here is an example of how a massive shift to Pathway 1 courage can have an impact in sport.

Matt Cameron is one of our key 2016 Olympic BMX prospects. However, in 2012 Matt was not even funded by High Performance Sport, let alone seen as a prospect for the London Olympic Games, or as a medal prospect for 2016. At international events he was regularly missing out on qualifying for the main events, finishing around 60th. During our work together, he identified his Pathway 1 philosophy of courage. He then had to prove he was living it. And live it he did!

Coinciding with a shift in his attitude, his performances skyrocketed, and he is now part of the core group of riders vying for spots at Rio in 2016. Most importantly, he is now fully funded by High Performance Sport as a result of his recent performances and can concentrate on his riding.

Here is a quote from Matt that beautifully describes what it is like to live with Pathway 1 courage and the power this generates.

PATHWAY 1 IS OFTEN LIVING 'UNCOMFORTABLE'!

Working from Pathway 1 has made me realise so many things. It pushed me into places that I never, ever thought or imagined I would be. If I had not lived Pathway 1 fully and felt this uncomfortable there is no way I would have succeeded or got even close to the point I am at now or the places to come.

Matt Cameron

Matt in 2013 sprint training in San Diego, California, USA.

In addition to his courage, Sir Edmund Hillary would have had a deep belief in his ability as a general climber, and trusted that if he prepared extremely well then he would be physically able to climb the mountain. Combining courage and self-belief would have fuelled Ed's potential and ultimately been the difference that allowed him to achieve what no other human had. That is Pathway 1: it is the royal road to uncovering your own life potential. Living by Pathway 1 over an extended period of time will result in your achieving outcomes you would have previously only fantasised about. Pathway 1 is that powerful, and when lived fully can give you the life you dream of immediately.

Tenzing Norgay and Edmund Hillary take a well-earned cup of tea en route to being the first men to climb Everest. I would like to think that when they strode through 27,997, 27,998, 27,999 and then 28,000 feet neither man would have been worried or afraid that they could die. In fact, I am sure they would have yelled their defiance at the mountain, challenging it to take them, and then charged through to 28,000 feet. That is how we should all live: from courage and never backing down to our self-doubts or fear of failing!

Another example of how Pathway 1 can be applied to sport with great results is golfer Mark Brown. When Mark shot 62 at Kingston Heath Golf Club to win the British Open Qualifying tournament in January 2013 and hit a course record, he was operating from pure Pathway 1 courage. He was absolutely committed to hitting his shots with brutal courage. Fear of playing badly or dropping shots did not even come into his mind. There was no fear or doubt, just the courage to play from a pure mind, and a deep commitment and determination to stick to his game plan.

In this mindset, the most important thing is to play from courage and to 'let go'; the result, good or bad, is of secondary importance. If you have a deep trust in yourself that you will play your best golf when your mind is like this, the result will take care of itself. Consequently, you can then just get on and hit the ball!

I asked Mark what was the key to the 62. He replied that during the entire round he worked hard at not caring about the outcome at all. He said his main goal for the round was to inject the LION, and to see how free he could be and how far he could take 'letting go', just playing from utter courage with no regard to the outcome, good or bad. It worked pretty well!

I also asked his caddie the same question. He replied: 'We spent the first nine holes chatting about fishing and beer with not one mention of or reflection on golf or his swing, which was the polar opposite to the day before, when he shot 72. He was six under par through nine at Kingston Heath; one of the best courses in the world. From the outside looking in, what I saw was a man playing with complete freedom and blatant disregard for outcome.

A scorer asked him what his score was after he pared the 15th hole and, as he started to give the score, he stopped, looked confused and then turned to me to ask how many under he was. He knew he was eight or nine but wasn't actually sure, which was a great sign from my point of view as he was still just charging and trying to play each hole as best he could.

Walking down 16 he turned to me and said, "Mate, starting to get a bit nervous. We could be going to the Open."

My reply was, "Who cares about the Open? Let's just keep playing. Anyway, what would DG say?"

To that Brownie replied, "Yeah, stuff it," and promptly hit a five iron to six feet and holed the putt to go 10 under.'

He shot 62, a record at a course that has hosted the best players in the world, including Tiger Woods, and he did it with complete freedom and disregard for outcome. Anyone walking in the group would have thought he was out on a Sunday afternoon with a couple of mates having a casual hit, not shooting 62 around one of the most revered courses in the world to qualify for a major championship.

Mark Brown's caddie's recollection of his 62 highlights what Pathway 1 looks like in golf and sport in general. It is acting from courage and belief to pursue what you want to have happen; for example, making the kick, sinking the putt, making a birdie or winning. It is never acting from fear or doubt, or in such a way as to try to avoid bad outcomes; for example, trying to avoid going out-of-bounds by aiming further and further away from trouble, or trying not to three-putt by tentatively lagging the ball up towards the hole. Pathway 1 is followed by the courageous person, irrespective of what they are doing (e.g. talking to their teacher, presenting to their boss or representing their country). Pathway 2 is followed by the careful coward – someone whose life is driven by fear of failure and self-doubt, and who does everything not to be judged or to upset others, or to fail!

DEEPENING OUR UNDERSTANDING OF HOW PATHWAY 1 IS APPLIED TO LIFE AND SPORT

We can now use Sir Edmund Hillary and Mark Brown's Pathway 1 examples to help understand how Pathway 1 relates to life and sport. The next section will use golf as the example. Golf provides such a great representation of how the mind works and how we need to apply the mind to get desired outcomes in any area of life. As you read through this example, you can replace golf with any sport you may be playing or any area of life (e.g. work or school projects). The same processes and principles apply. The mind works the same across settings, whether you are on the sporting field, at the café with a friend, sitting a school final exam or presenting to your boss.

For example, a right-handed golfer who recently started to live from Pathway 1 is standing on the par five fourth hole at St Andrews Golf Club in Hamilton. The hole has OB and a river down the right. Historically this golfer would have been terrified of holes like this, and would have aimed way left in order to take away the risk of going OB right. Ironically, he would often still go OB right despite his attempts to 'run away' from his fear.

THE PAR FIVE FOURTH AT ST ANDREWS IN HAMILTON

The par five fourth at St Andrews Golf course in Hamilton New Zealand is a classic hole where players who fade the ball fear going OB well before they even get there. On this hole there is no shot if you go left, and you OB into the river if you go right. It looks like there is plenty of space down the middle, but as you can

> see from the second photo, the hole funnels to a tight bottleneck about 60 metres out from an extremely difficult two-tiered green, making things very interesting indeed.

Eventually, the golfer had enough. He started to feel sick and tired of the self-doubt and fear of going OB that would seep into his mind from the moment he arrived at the course and increase in intensity the closer he got to the hole. He began to develop the courage to change his mindset. As part of his evolving Pathway 1 plan to play golf to his full potential and master holes like the fourth at St Andrews, he decided to see a golf coach for assistance to learn how to draw the ball.

He became absolutely committed to mastering this shot and practised whenever he could. His weekly schedule showed his commitment and how fully he was 'paying the price'. He also committed to embracing the risk of failing by playing every hole with OB right using his new draw, and accepting that for a time he would probably go OB a fair bit. He knew, however, that if he kept following the plan, in a short time he would start playing the best golf of his life. All it really meant was that, for a while, he would need to take more golf balls with him!

When he stands behind the ball on this particular day and looks down the hole, he thinks the following thoughts: 'I am the LION!' 'Pathway 1.' 'I live on the edge of my potential sunshine.' 'I will play on the edge of bogey and OB because I play my best there.' 'I don't care about my score or going OB . . . what I care most about is that I play from courage!'

If thoughts of OB or dropping shots come into his mind, then he replaces them with thoughts such as: 'I would rather fail from a strong place than ever succeed from a weak one.' 'I will not let fear control me.' 'Now be strong!' Or even: 'I will not be a coward!' All of these phrases reflect strong self-talk, but are far more than just that because they tap into powerful Pathway 1 courage, and as a result inspire the player to embrace the fear of failing on his terms.

If at any point his mind or body tries to take over his Pathway 1 decision to 'play on the edge of going OB' and make him aim further away from the OB 'just to be safe', his true Pathway 1 mindset will grab back control and aim even further over the OB, thereby confronting his fear and intentionally inviting what he most fears.

If the fear continues and the golfer starts to aim more and more left again, despite having already tried to deal with his fear and doubt, as a true Pathway 1 golfer he will hit it out of bounds on purpose to take back control.

He will then take the penalty, reload and hit again, until he hits the shot he wants. He will be prepared to hit many balls OB because it is more important for him to live from courage than to be a coward and give in to his fear by aiming well away from trouble. He will then fill out the actual score for that hole on the card and write a note to the handicapper not to adjust the score because the 19, or whatever score he took, reflected his true ability in that moment. Deep down he will not care what his score or handicap ended up being because it is more important to him and his integrity to play from courage. He will feel great pride for not having backed down to fear and cowardice.

Pride is a critical emotion for you to feel. It is a direct emotional reaction to acting from courage. When golfers come to see me with self-doubt or low confidence issues I do not even talk to them about that. We look for places where they are acting from fear and we then build plans for them to act courageously. They get an automatic increase in self-belief and confidence simply from acting from courage, because that is how the mind is wired to work, and hence why living Pathway 1 makes you feel so alive!

Further, increasing pride deepens self-acceptance, another automatic emotional process. With increasing self-acceptance you care less what others think about you. The benefits of deep self-acceptance are huge and can't be emphasised enough. The main reason golfers tense up and repress rather than relax, express and embrace the challenge of the game is because they worry about what others will think of them, and especially what others will think of their score and handicap. Getting caught up with what your score and handicap are reflects a lack of self-acceptance in that it highlights that you need others to think a certain way about you to feel good or like yourself. Here is a great little self-acceptance story from Hana Seifert, a promising young New Zealand amateur golfer.

THE DIRECT LINK BETWEEN SELF-ACCEPTANCE AND PERFORMING UNDER PRESSURE: MY SELF-ACCEPTANCE HOLE

It was the second round of the Australian Amateur Championship and everything was going to plan. I had played 12 holes and stepped onto the 13th tee, a tight but short par four with trees right and bunkers left. It didn't need a driver and I was sticking with the game plan, which was to hit five wood. I had gone through my normal pre-shot routine and I was feeling great. Next minute . . .

I was holding my finish watching this golf ball go straight into the Australian snake-ridden bunda right in front of the tee: something between a drop kick and a top! My playing partners probably wanted to laugh, and I didn't know whether to laugh or cry! But there was nothing I could do except try to find my ball! The spectators that were helping me look for my ball kept saying, 'Even I could have done better than this.'

At this stage I was still reasonably calm, but as time ticked by I felt a bit of a panic starting to build up. I found my ball and, to top things off, it was on a dusty, stony path and there was nothing on the rules sheet about whether you got a drop or not. So I needed a referee!

Well . . . the referee may as well have been back in New Zealand – it felt like it took him that long to get to me! Meanwhile, there were groups backing up on the tee (which I was only about 60 metres away from). And this was when I was hit with

Hana playing the Australian Amateur at Riversdale Golf Club in 2013.

pure self-acceptance. I knew that previously I would've started pacing around, getting flustered and frustrated, not to mention embarrassed that I was holding up the entire field and they were probably thinking, 'Who is this girl?' But I genuinely didn't care! I just thought to myself that this was the perfect opportunity to test my self-acceptance. I waved the groups behind me on the tee through and I stood and looked at them as they walked past with their quizzical looks, and I just thought to myself, 'Yes, I have just hit it here, and I do not care what you think!'

Even when the referee eventually turned up and opened with, 'Oh, wow. I've never seen someone hit it here before,' I just continued my 'hooo hummm' relaxation and felt no emotion or embarrassment. I simply did not care, in the most positive sort of way. I went on to stiff the next shot to a foot and make the best bogey of my life!

Hana Seifert

Playing with a mindset of self-acceptance, a good work ethic and good coaching will see any golfer play better golf almost immediately. Further, in a very short time, they will end up uncovering their golfing potential. Perhaps most important though, they will deeply enjoy their golf. All this comes from playing from courage.

Getting back to the golfer I was describing earlier, as he stands on the par five, he is the master of his own golfing destiny. He is in no way influenced or controlled by fear of a bad outcome, or desperation to look like a good golfer in front of his peers. In fact he is open to failing and his handicap going out in order to live from courage and hold true to Pathway 1.

Inspiring philosophy, isn't it? That is how you know you are really living Pathway 1: when you feel pure, invigorated, free and inspired. You feel alive, and golf, or whatever sport you are playing, becomes a whole new experience because of it.

When golfers enter a pure Pathway 1 mindset, fear and doubt melt away and are replaced by a deep excitement and courage to live on the edge of their potential. With more and more success over time the courage is then mixed with a deep certainty and belief that they will execute the certain shot they are planning. They accept that there will be times when things may not go to plan and that their handicaps may even go out, but they trust deeply that by holding to their path things will work out better than they ever imagined in the long run.

This is exactly the same in all areas of life. Living from Pathway 1 in the way shown in the golf example above will unleash your mind to 'act' from deep courage, whatever it is that you are doing. It is this 'unleashing' that engages your unconscious instinct and you just 'do', rather than thinking about doing. It is the thinking about what you are doing that can make everything fall apart at the seams. Through instinct, the unconscious mind is able to release your body to do what it is that you have prepared it to do. As a result, individual athletes, teams and people can do the most amazing things. This is when the magic happens!

The following is a brief passage from former All Black rugby halfback Brendon Leonard, highlighting how an athlete is able to 'just play' with a Pathway 1 mindset. Brendon surged into the All Blacks in 2007 after a super rugby season characterised by unpredictable instinctual runs. For those who love rugby, they were pure moments of magic.

THE FREEDOM TO JUST PLAY!

A Pathway 1 state of mind meant I ran onto the field not trying to please anyone, but rather with the freedom to play the game I wanted to play. I was not concerned with making mistakes, or being ridiculed for poor decisions after the game. I just did not care. I always felt I played my best when the mistakes didn't matter, and the good things I did stayed in my memory a lot longer. I believe if you can enter the game with a clear frame of mind, meaning the only thing you are thinking about is going onto the field and playing your game and not caring what external

A great shot of Brendon 'Harry' Leonard in full flight against the Blues in 2011 at the Waikato Rugby Stadium.

influences might think, then you will tap into your instinct and find your true potential!

Brendon Leonard

GENERATING A PATHWAY 1 PHILOSOPHY

The first step in building a Pathway 1 philosophy is to come up with a phrase that best expresses what Pathway 1 will look like for you. This will be a phrase that your life will come to represent. It is the way people will describe your life when they talk about you at your funeral. It is what will be written on your tombstone when you are buried! When looking back over your life, people should be able to see the link between all your successes and your Pathway 1 philosophy (i.e. how the Pathway 1 philosophy resulted in those successes). It will be that important. It is the anchor we will frequently link to throughout this book.

If you were working with me individually, I would frequently challenge you to prove to me that you were living by the philosophy as well as playing your sport by it. This would become our number one goal, and it would be far more important to me than any of your results. The continuation of our work together would be dependent upon your ongoing commitment to living this way. I would rather work with someone who was fully living their Pathway 1 philosophy but ranked number 3000 in the world, than a current world champion who was choosing not to live from courage. It is that important to me!

I know that if you can master living and playing sport, or whatever it is you are pursuing through your Pathway 1 philosophy, the results will take care of themselves. It is far more important to challenge yourself to inject your philosophy into your game than it is to try to play well. Mastering your philosophy rather than worrying about trying to be perfect is the key to results beyond your wildest dreams!

For example, I mentioned earlier what I thought Sir Ed's

Pathway 1 philosophy would have been. Here are some other ways of wording his philosophy:

- 'I would rather fail from a strong place than ever succeed from a weak one.'
- 'I will choose to live when others choose to curl up and die.'
- 'Courage.'
- 'Live on the edge of your potential.'
- 'Live on the edge of bogey or birdie!' (for golf)
- 'Be the LION!'
- 'Be the honey badger!' (If you do not know what a honey badger is, go and look up 'A tribute to the honey badger' on YouTube; you will immediately see why this is listed here.)

You can see how each of these philosophies would inspire a person to behave courageously and live with full expression. That is what a great Pathway 1 philosophy does. It becomes a blueprint for how you live your life in every domain. Pathway 1 should be immediately obvious in someone's behaviour, decisions and actions. That is the key. Others must be able to see your Pathway 1 philosophy in your day-to-day decisions and actions right now, not tomorrow or next week, and it should be apparent in all areas of your life. It should be obvious in your interactions with your family and your partner, if you have one, with your boss at work, etc.

The examples above fulfil these requirements. A person living from these philosophies would appear to be vastly different creatures from those living from self-doubt and fear of failure, or what I refer to as Pathway 2.

Mark Brown's Pathway 1 philosophy is: 'Be the LION!'

Lisa Carrington's is: 'I will choose to live when others choose to curl up and die.'

They both strive to bring their respective philosophies into every part of their lives, not just their sport.

PATHWAY 1: EXERCISE 2

Generate Your Own Pathway 1 Philosophy

Now it is time to build your Pathway 1 Philosophy of Courage. Do not rush it if you cannot come up with one straight away. This is a critical step, and one that takes some athletes a while to do. For example, one athlete was driving when they uncovered theirs and pulled over to text it. It was:

'Practise and play like your life depends upon it, because it does!'

Write yours here:

Now go and sit down with your coach, parent(s), partner or spouse and discuss your Pathway 1 philosophy with them. As part of that discussion, agree together what your final Pathway 1 will be.

When you are all happy with your Pathway 1 philosophy, write it down somewhere you will see it often: on the bathroom mirror, on the fridge, above the door in your room, on the door in your room, on both sides of the door, on the ceiling in your room! The more you commit to your new philosophy publicly and with your significant others, the more 'healthy' pressure it puts on you to live it.

PATHWAY 1: EXERCISE 3
Injecting Your Pathway 1 Philosophy of Courage into Your Life

Now you have a strong Pathway 1 philosophy, you are going to figure out what it would look like in action and put it to work immediately. You are creating a blueprint for yourself to follow, no matter what area you are reading this book to help with (e.g. school, sport, relationships, finances, etc).

To get the greatest benefit from your Pathway 1 philosophy you must live by it in the most important areas of your life. Choose the two or three most important things in your life (e.g. partner, friends, finances, work, university, school, music, sport) and answer the following question for each one.

What would **absolute courage** look like in _____?

For example: What would **absolute courage** look like in maths?

The answer may be strategies such as:
- making an appointment with my teacher
- clarifying what the end point will look like and what sort of equations I need to be able to solve
- establishing a clear plan for how I will achieve the ability to do those equations
- arriving first to class
- asking the teacher at the end of each session exactly what homework is required
- setting up a homework system that forces me to do half an hour of maths every night
- asking questions in class
- asking for extra homework
- asking for extra tuition prior to exams.

Another example could be: What would **absolute courage** look like in relation to my business or work?

The answer may be strategies such as:
- sitting down with my boss and writing a performance development plan
- approaching the most respected person in my field and region to be my mentor
- dressing like I have already become super successful
- enrolling for a public speaking course at Toast Masters
- putting my name forward for a big project at work even though it petrifies me
- organising weekly meetings with my boss to look at my performance across the week
- videoing all my interviews with customers
- getting all my clients to complete satisfaction feedback sheets after each consultation.

Every one of these strategies relies on courage to get yourself to act in a certain manner in order to achieve a certain desired outcome. It is the consistent acting from courage, day in and day out, week after week and month after month, that in turn causes your life to turn out a certain way. Imagine acting out the strategies above over a three-month and then nine-month period. Your achievement in maths would rise to levels you would have never thought possible. At work, your skill level, confidence, potential, career and bank balance would explode. The most successful people in any area of life do these kinds of strategies. Their success is directly linked to their behaviours, and has nothing to do with how smart they are.

Write or list here what your Pathway 1 Philosophy of Courage would look like in the two or three areas of your life that you decided to focus on above:

_____

_____

_____

When you have put your lists together for the two or three most important areas in your life (or the one critical area if you chose a single area), discuss it with your key people (e.g. your coach, parent(s), partner or spouse) to see what they think and whether you are on the right track. They may have a couple of courage behaviours they want you to add to your lists. In the end, you will have a Pathway 1 code that will be critical to you achieving your life potential and dreams, whatever they may be.

THE PATHWAY 1 GOLDEN RULES

There are some golden rules to embracing Pathway 1 fully, which are listed below. As you read through them, reflect on how fully you live by these rules. Give yourself a score out of 10 for each; 10 out of 10 should be your goal!

1. **Pathway 1 is about embracing failing, by pushing limits and thereby living on the edge of your potential, not short of it.** Pathway 1 is ironically about failing more than it is about succeeding. It is about living in a space where the pursuit of your potential is far more important than how good you can get or how rich you can become. In this mindset, failing becomes success. Crazy, I know, but it is true. It is thrilling to think we can get our minds there, and we can! Living with this incredibly high risk of failing makes you initially uncomfortable, but later, when you ingrain Pathway 1 into your character, it becomes exciting, as you can't wait to see your growth. If you are uncomfortable or excited and feel like you are right on the edge of failing (i.e. your potential)

you are living Pathway 1. If you are comfortable or cruising, then you are living Pathway 2, and if you dig around in your mind a little bit you will eventually find that you are living in the comfort zone because deep down you actually fear failing. Once your mind makes this critical connection, watch your potential fly! Here is a world-class reflection by New Zealand Silver Fern Laura Langman about the importance of embracing failing in order to truly succeed. The photo Laura provided was a perfect fit for this golden rule as well. She was certainly flying compared to her Australian opposition!

THE POWER OF EMBRACING FAILING

> Pathway 1 has taught me that failing breeds success; failing is to be celebrated, not feared. My perspective of Pathway 1 is an attitude that every day is an opportunity to be better than I was the day before in all facets of life, as I strive to achieve my Impossible Dream; consequently I fail often. Living in this space has taught me that embracing pressure and disregarding the outcome results in my greatest successes.
>
> **Laura Langman**

2. **Pathway 1 has both human and performance values.** Sir Ed received a civil funeral not only because he climbed Mt Everest and drove a Massey Ferguson tractor to the South Pole, but because he was such a decent human being. It was his compassion and generosity towards people that won him love and respect. His performance values, such as valuing adventure, pushing personal limits and enjoying competition, led him to the summit of Everest. Without both performance and human values, you are not living by Pathway 1. Some people think they are living by Pathway 1 but hold only selfish, me-first values without a sense of respect and compassion for others. Selfishness is a sign that someone is living by Pathway 2; they may still end up being successful, but eventually they will be very unhappy, and unfortunately will make others around them (e.g. family) unhappy too. The importance of living a value-based life cannot be understated! Those who do not live by values live by urges, and living an urge-controlled life is fraught with risk and frequently ends up with difficulties (e.g. gambling, excessive drinking and ruined marriages). To demonstrate how critical this point is, I have included comments from two very special people who, for me, do live by values. It has been really pleasing to see them do so well.

   The first comment is from Luke Toomey, a promising

up-and-coming New Zealand amateur golfer. He highlights the importance of strong personal values as the foundation to a powerful Pathway 1 mindset. The second comment is from heptathlete Sarah Cowley, who represented New Zealand at the 2012 London Olympic games. She reflects on the enormous impact connecting with her values has on the quality of her life experience.

THE LINK BETWEEN VALUES AND PERFORMANCE

Living and challenging myself to hold true to my Pathway 1 philosophy has helped me realise how important it is to have strong values. When I began working with David, he asked me to write a list of 'core values' and find those attributes that I thought would be essential in achieving my dream. To begin with I had a list of twelve values ranging from determination to trustworthiness. We then reduced these until I settled on four: generosity, humility, honesty and ruthlessness.

I believe becoming 'the best' is a habit that manifests itself

through daily practise of your values through any activity both on and off the golf course. When I incorporate an equal balance of all four of my values, it allows me to feel content and calm, and from that, I feel as though I can be the best at anything I put my mind to.

Luke Toomey

Getting clear about my core values has had a huge impact on my performance and on my life. It's easy just to pass through your days thinking you know what's important to you – tricking yourself that you are giving your time and energy to your values. The reality is that living your values is a journey, which requires work. It certainly was and still is for me one of the most rewarding tasks I have ever done.

As the distinction of my core values grew so did my performance and ultimately my self-acceptance. I was free to unleash at another level. Ironically, despite wanting to compete at the Olympic Games for a long time, I got so much more satisfaction from the journey through my campaign than something I'd dreamed about for 20 years! I jumped higher than I thought was possible simply because I think I was at peace with myself. I was pure.

Sarah Cowley

3. **Pathway 1 is characterised by attention to detail and meticulous planning.** Pure Pathway 1 athletes train and practice today for many months or years in front of them. A top Olympian, for example, trains today for four years' time. Jesse Owens, who won four gold medals in the 1936 Berlin Olympics said, 'A lifetime of training for just 10 seconds!' If you live in the here and now and practise only to try to get a perfect outcome right now, then you are living Pathway 2. If you practise living on the edge of your potential and are driven by a deep desire to learn something right now, today, that will help you perform in the long term, and are therefore accepting the risk of failing in the now, then you are living Pathway 1. If you are also young enough, it is very likely that you will go on to become one of the greatest in whatever arena you perform in.
4. **Pathway 1 demands high self-accountability. This is achieved when you live by the following four non-negotiable rules:**
(a) You are honest with yourself and others – no excuses.
(b) You do what is right; you take the hard road – no giving up and no whining.
(c) You generate your own proof that you are good enough to reach the dream – no reassurance seeking.
(d) You give everything to the dream and expect nothing in return – live by humility!

In summary, many people never take the time to think about how they live their lives. Most spend every day trying to make enough money to pay their next set of bills or rent, or keep up with their mortgage. They spend their lives waiting to be able to retire and live the good life. Many young adults still at school never really take the time to reflect on what sort of person they want to be, and spend most of their time worrying what others think of them and trying to fit in. They cram for exams and hope that they have done enough to get through. Unfortunately, many of these people don't change during their lifetime and end up reaching old age full of regrets that they have not done all the things they fantasised of doing.

The key to living the life you deeply desire and to reaching old age absolutely content is to live life to the full. It does not mean you should be stupid in how you approach it and never plan for tomorrow. It does not mean that you should take unnecessary risks. In fact it means quite the opposite. When I say 'live life to the full' I mean pay great attention to detail and have elaborate long- and short-term plans that leave nothing to chance, and put everything under your control. It does not mean things will always work out, but funnily enough often they do; and when they do not, you must simply brush yourself off, get back on the horse and get back to work. Failing should no longer have a powerful negative emotional hold on you. In fact, failing can be incredibly exciting because it often means you are living and playing on the edge of your potential and great success is just around the corner!

A pure Pathway 1 philosophy will live on long after you have gone, and it will become a powerful legacy that inspires not only your family, but all who knew you. Quite possibly, if you end up living a philosophy like Ed Hillary, you will inspire a nation!

Establishing a pure, meaningful Pathway 1 philosophy is critically important, and that is why I started with it in this book. Make sure you take the time to do the process justice and do a thorough job of it. Getting it right and establishing a philosophy with great personal meaning to you will unlock a deep energy and power that you will possibly have never experienced before, one that leaves you feeling like you can achieve anything you set your mind to. Then once that energy is ignited, all you need is direction, and that comes next!

'TO GET WHAT YOU HAVE NEVER HAD, YOU ARE GOING TO HAVE TO DO WHAT YOU HAVE NEVER DONE!'

MAC ANDERSON

PATHWAY 1 AND THE IMPOSSIBLE DREAM

Connecting with your Pathway 1 philosophy is a critical step in unleashing your deep potential in life and achieving your greatest goals, whether it is at school, at work, applying for your next job or asking the woman or man of your dreams out for a coffee.

If you live from a Pathway 1 perspective, you can guarantee the job you go for will be your dream job and the woman or man you ask out will be your dream partner. You will never settle for second best again. You will never apply for a job that is almost what you are after, or ask out a person who is just 'good enough'. Exciting prospects lie ahead.

I used the word 'dream' in the last paragraph several times, and for a reason. When I talk about linking in with a long-term goal from Pathway 1, I am not referring to what most people think of as goals or long-term objectives. These are set later when establishing the strategic plan to success. Usually when people talk about long-term goal setting the first thing they say is that it's important to keep it 'realistic'. I cannot stand that word or that way of thinking about long-term goals, visions or dreams. I think it is critical to stay 'real world' focused when reflecting on your work ethic and day-by-day habits, and how hard are you working. But outside that, I encourage you to watch out for any thinking that tells you to be 'realistic' when setting long-term goals. The risk of this thinking is that you will never push your limits. Imagine if Sir Ed had listened to 'realistic' thinking from scientists – he would have never attempted Everest!

When I talk about Pathway 1 goal setting, I am talking about something very special and powerful. It is the next critical step to unleashing your true potential and is the focus of this chapter. Through it, you can achieve the 'Impossible Dream'. I will expand on what I mean by 'impossible' shortly, but in essence Pathway 1 goal setting will force you to '**LI**ve **O**utside **N**ormality' (**LION** – great acronym!) It is choosing to be a LION or LIONess, not a lamb.

Treasure discussions and thoughts you have about your impossible dream. The exercise or process of uncovering your greatest dream is a critical step in achieving it. Most people, however, simply never get clear on what the end point really is, let alone what it looks like or how to get there. Many say they want to be rich, or be the best in the world at this or that. Often these statements are just empty words that blow away in the wind as soon as they are said. There is no substance behind the words, and certainly no courage or belief. People might say them because they think they are what others want them to say or want to hear, or what will impress others. Often these statements are merely fantasy: at no point do these people actually mean what they are saying!

I have found that most people, and historically myself included, have no idea where they want to be in life and simply meander through it, making decisions in the moment, here and there along the way. Further, most people end up making decisions based on emotions – usually fear of failure and self-doubt, and an unconscious desperation to be comfortable and secure. Making decisions this way is often costly. For example, making decisions from desperation in relationships or jobs can cost five to ten years of someone's life, or in some cases even longer (e.g. marrying the wrong person or investing in the wrong profession or company).

During my many years working across various elite sports, there is probably only a handful of athletes I saw who exhibited a real, deep and meaningful connection to a dream. Sure, there were many who were incredibly successful, but most of them had 'sort of just ended up' being good at their sport and therefore carried on doing what they did because they were good at it, not because they were deeply passionate about what they did. None of the athletes who were 'just doing' their sport, I believe, ever exhibited that real 'magic' you see when a deeply driven athlete reaches peak performance. Consequently, many never reached their potential; they merely became good enough, and because they were not 'living the dream' were also often very unhappy.

When one of the very few who were deeply in touch with and connected to a meaningful dream told me about it, it felt as though their achieving the dream was an absolute certainty. It was special to hear something so big and seemingly impossible to achieve said as an absolute truth, as if there was nothing else for them, no other option but to succeed. It was what I refer to as one of those 'Goose Bump Moments'.

Perhaps what is most special about this sort of mindset is that when a person deeply and genuinely links with a powerful dream and commits their life to achieving it, a sense of trust and contentment settles over their mind. It is as though they reach a place where the outcome actually no longer matters. At a deeper level, it seems that what has become most important is that they believe in themselves and live that way along the journey to the end point, not the actual outcome. What others think or say no longer becomes relevant. When you connect absolutely to something and 'cut off' your mind from all other possibilities, you achieve a deep sense of patience and calm, almost as though the mind is saying, 'OK, this is it, this is what I will do till I die!' As a result, they are not enticed by different opportunities along the way; there is only one thing they desire. Achieving this sort of peaceful yet powerful mindset is very special.

Not surprisingly, the athletes who genuinely connect with their deepest dreams end up dropping into a space where they just utterly love what they do, and they do it just for the sake of doing it. There is no expectation of performance or having to reach the dream, only a deep knowledge that they are now embarking on a lifetime commitment to this pursuit. These athletes present like they have married their sport and married their dream. There is no need to motivate these athletes to train and practise; you cannot keep them off the court or away from the field. They cannot stop thinking about their dream, and ironically that often becomes a problem. Here is a good example from perhaps one of New Zealand's most unknown up-and-coming young golfers, Will Monery.

ABSOLUTE LOVE OF THE GAME

Roughly three years ago, I got an email from a young man asking to meet me and talk about developing his mind. I gave him a time I could see him for 30 minutes at the NZ High Performance Sport Training Centre café in Auckland. He said he would be there. I walked down the stairs at 4.25 p.m. and there was a young man sitting with his grandfather. We went through the normal introductions and greetings. When I asked him how school had gone that day, he replied, 'Very well, thank you.' I then asked him where he went to school – it was in Wellington, at the other end of the North Island! He had finished early, at 1 p.m., to catch a flight to Auckland. His grandfather had then picked him up and driven

him to the other side of the city for our half-hour session. He was going to fly back to Wellington after our meeting.

His dream was to become the greatest golfer in the world – a perfect dream! Cutting this story short, Will is now 18 years old, and is not just playing golf in Wellington like most young people his age who say they have the same dream might be. He has secured a university scholarship to play golf in Florida, USA. Will has never played national-level golf in New Zealand, but has already made the university's five-man team in his first year! For those of you who know the world of golf, that is an enormous achievement.

This brings me to the key part of this story. I recently got an email from Will asking for advice. He had a problem that was worrying him. He could not stop thinking about golf during his lectures. He said that all he wanted to do when he woke up was to play golf, and all he could think about when he was with friends, or in lectures was golf, and he wanted to check if it was normal! I quickly replied to the email, telling him that it was exactly what I wanted, that in fact it was an incredibly promising sign, and he should allow his passionate obsession to run wild.

As you connect with your deepest dream during this next section, I want you to remind yourself to appreciate the enormity of what you are saying and committing to. Only then will you move towards being one of those very few people I described above. It would be easy to rush through this section and give it little, if any, real deep thought and consideration. For example, you could simply write a big dream down on paper and tick it off as done. If you are going to do that, then I suggest closing this book and just getting on with how you have always lived your life because nothing is going to change. You will still be the same person in five years as you are today! That may sound quite harsh, but that is how I am. I will not sugar-coat anything. I will tell you things as they are, and if I think you are wasting your time, I will let you know.

By taking time to really think about your dream and find the exact words to represent it, you will be honouring yourself and all you are as a person. It will also send an enormous message to your mind that you are deadly serious, and are already an outstanding person in your own right, no matter what your pursuit. For example, you could be an accomplished pianist at 16 years old. Your dream could be to study music in New York and revolutionise the way the piano is played. By genuinely connecting to this dream, you will send powerful messages to your mind that you are already an outstanding musician and that your potential is unlimited – critical messages for your mind to accept. This would be the same if you had never played an instrument, but had the dream of playing the guitar in the school band. It all starts with a genuine linking to what you deeply want to achieve, and not settling for second best, or what you think others want you to do. Linking deeply with your dream, and the underlying reason you want to achieve it is vitally important to unleashing your mind. Take your time.

The dream must sound 'impossible' and be totally unrealistic! Sir Edmund Hillary never set a long-term goal he had even the slightest idea he could achieve! Most goal-setting advice is the opposite of this. It strongly suggests that you live in 'reality' and set 'smart goals'. This is a massive mistake. Remember how every scientist agreed that the 'reality' was that Mt Everest could not be climbed. If Sir Edmund had listened to that reality he would have never even attempted to climb it!

> **'WE DIDN'T KNOW IF IT WAS HUMANLY POSSIBLE TO REACH THE TOP OF MT EVEREST.'**
> SIR EDMUND HILLARY

How often do you limit yourself by being locked into reality? Sadly most people live by the reality rule and consequently never make anything of their lives because they never try. If you ever read a goal-setting sheet that tells you to base long-term goals on reality, screw it up and throw it in the trash! If you ever have a teacher or psychologist tell you that long-term goals and dreams must be realistic, ask them to explain why people like Sir Edmund Hillary, Nelson Mandela and Martin Luther King did not follow the same ideas.

Let's expand on what I mean by 'Impossible Dream'. For a dream to be true to Pathway 1, it must sound impossible. This does not mean that it must be physically impossible, although it could be, it means that it will sound impossible to most people you tell. I often use Sir Edmund Hillary's Everest dream to highlight what I mean by the Impossible Dream. The Impossible Dream reflects a dream that most other people would tell you was not possible. I explain to players that if your mind or someone in your family or anyone on the street tells you that what you want to do is impossible, then you will have identified the perfect dream!

Connecting with a deep, genuine, meaningful, Impossible Dream sets the Pathway 1 mindset in concrete. Remember,

Pathway 1 is the pathway of courage and being uncomfortable. Publicly verbalising a true Pathway 1 dream requires great courage because of the judgemental response you will get from people. Linking with a dream this big will make you incredibly uncomfortable because of the very real risk that you will not achieve it.

As already mentioned, living from courage does wonderful things for your mind. It will trigger off a powerful automatic response that results in pride. Pride is the foundation emotion for self-acceptance; self-acceptance is critical for self-belief; self-belief is critical for self-confidence; and all of these are critical for enthusiasm and ambition. Enthusiasm and ambition are important motivators to get you out of bed in the morning, especially when things may not be going so well with your sport, music, school or work.

The difference between a successful and unsuccessful person will come down to how many quality minutes they spend practising, training and performing what they do; especially right after they have failed or succeeded, times when many people do less. It will be the robustness that comes from evolving a Pathway 1 mindset that will lead to you doing more than anyone else in the world who has the same dream. If your sport or pursuit is golf, for example, and your dream is to become the world number one, there will be millions more like you around the globe who have the same dream.

All too often, humans limit their potential before they even set sail on a certain life course by aiming for a low goal that they have a good idea they will achieve. It seems to be more mentally and socially acceptable, in New Zealand anyhow, to aim low and hope that we will achieve high. This is the 'safe' route and one that protects people from social scrutiny and judgement. I struggle with that approach to life. I aim to teach all the players and athletes I work with, and my children, that it is acceptable and expected to aim impossibly high. It is not about aiming high so that if you fail you will end up better off. Operating from Pathway 1 is about aiming high, having deep courage to plan to get there, and then paying the price required to reach your target (or you die from old age!) The thought of not reaching the dream does not even enter into consciousness. If doubt does come into a person's mind that they may not reach their dream, ironically their response will be, 'I actually don't care! What I care more about is that I commit my heart and soul to the project and commit absolutely everything to achieving what is deeply important to me!' This is very similar to my earlier suggestion about what Sir Edmund Hillary would have said to himself when his mind considered the possibility that he could die attempting Everest.

IMPOSSIBLE DREAM SETTING: EXERCISE 1

Write your Impossible Dream here in as much detail as you need to really give it some deep meaning:

Share your dream with your family, parents, partner or spouse. It is vital that you share it with those closest to you. You are not going to be able to achieve it by yourself. Make sure they know that they will play a critical part in you reaching your dream.

Courage Test

Now you have your dream clearly set, it is important to check that it is an 'Impossible Dream'. The next time someone asks you what your long-term goal or dream is, make sure you tell them! You can choose to take this experiment as far as you like. For example, you could find a complete stranger, somebody in your class at school or at your work and tell them your dream. If they say that it is impossible, laugh at you or ask if you are serious, then you have indeed identified an Impossible Dream. Well done! Do not under any circumstances change it now.

THE POWER OF BELIEVING IN THE 'IMPOSSIBLE'

Sarah Cowley's story is a fantastic example of the power that comes from connecting to a pure dream. Objective facts and other people's views said her goal for London was impossible. Therefore, her mind had to smash all the mental limitations she had set upon herself about what she was capable of achieving, to believe that anything was possible. The new universe she stepped into was sensational. The greatest impact I observed was not in her performance, which was exceptional in its own right, but the way that she started to embrace living fully. That was and still is far more important to me in all my work with athletes and teams than them actually winning a gold medal. In all honesty, I care little for the gold medal, but care very deeply about people achieving purity in their lives.

Your dream must sound incredibly clear, concise and inspiring, and be written and spoken in 'I will' language. An athlete living from Pathway 1 will sound very different from one who is living from Pathway 2 when establishing ultimate desired outcome. When I ask a person who is living Pathway 1 to tell me about their dream I get a clear, specific and detailed picture and plan. It will have been thought about often and over a long period of time. It is this quality that makes a Pathway 1 dream stand out compared to a Pathway 2 long-term goal or fantasy.

You will also find that your personal response to someone else's Pathway 1 dream compared to a Pathway 2 dream will contrast just as strongly. A Pathway 1 dream will inspire you. It will lift your spirits and your own sense of possibility. It will lead you to reflect on your own life and dreams and will propel you into action.

A person living from Pathway 1 with a deep pure dream will say something like this to me:

> 'My dream is to be the world number one by the time I am __ years old!'

They will then very likely get their plan out of their bag and show me. They might, for example, get their grandfather to come in and tell me how the family is right behind them and how he absolutely believes his grandson or granddaughter will make it. When I ask them 'Do you believe that?' They will first look at me sideways because they will think the question is nonsense, and then respond:

'Yes, I do absolutely believe I WILL be the world number one!'

If they are even slightly anti-social, they will tell me that was a stupid question, or they will get up and leave!

I then ask people, 'What if you fail and do not achieve your dream?' This question is just to test their mental toughness and resolve around their dream, and to see if they are 100 per cent committed to it. I am not intentionally being a disbeliever!

The answer I am looking for is along the lines of the following examples (and it will vary, depending on the person's character):

'Then I was wrong!'

'I am choosing to live every day believing I will achieve my dream. Living this way is more important than the outcome itself. I will achieve it or I won't. What is fully in my control is how I live each day, so I am going to choose to believe!'

'I am struggling with your question: are you saying that I should live every day believing that I won't achieve my dream? Sorry, I cannot accept that sort of mindset!'

Something incredibly powerful happens when a person deeply connects with a meaningful dream and thinks and talks about it from this mindset. It loads their mind with absolute will power to do whatever it takes to make it happen. It provides the mental strength to push through the tough times or any adversity that comes their way. They seem to accept that any setbacks are normal and to be expected. They don't cry or whine; they just deal with them and get on with it. It is as though there is another force that operates within the world that most people never discover. People who connect with an Impossible Dream tap into this energy source and they make their destiny happen!

IMPOSSIBLE DREAM SETTING: EXERCISE 2

It is critical to write and say your dream using 'I WILL' language, and to plan how you will answer the various questions you will inevitably get asked by people, such as the media, when you tell them your dream.

Rewrite your Impossible Dream here in 'I WILL' language.

E.g. I WILL be the greatest _____ ! I WILL win_____.

Now go through each of the following questions and write out in full what you will say when answering them. From now on, this is how you will sound. You will need to practise these in front of the mirror to get used to saying them.

Question 1: What is your long-term dream?
Answer:

_____

_____

_____

Question 2: Come on [journalist giggling], that is a really big dream! Do you truly believe you will achieve that?
Answer:

_____

_____

_____

Question 3: What if you do not achieve your dream?
Answer:

Not setting a Pathway 1 dream results in a vicious cycle of self-doubt and fear of failing.

Now let us look at what happens if someone sets a long-term goal from Pathway 2, or from a self-doubt and fear-of-failure mindset. If a person is Pathway 2, I will often hear a long and painfully deep silence when I ask them, 'What is your life dream?' Then I may hear a few 'ums', and finally I will hear a socially practised and middle-of-the-road statement such as, 'To make a lot of money' or 'To earn a living from my sport.'

These are great goals, but do not represent a Pathway 1, Sir Edmund Hillary, deep, Impossible Dream, and as a result will never tap into the powerful and unlimited energy that lies deep within our minds. It is then unlikely that people setting Pathway 2 long-term goals and targets will ever reach their true potential. They may still become good at whatever they do, even great, but their potential will remain untapped, and when they retire and look back over their life, deep down they will know it. They will feel regret, and they will know that they have simply gone through the motions of life. Any success will be experienced as hollow and unfulfilling because they could have uncovered something special and achieved so much more.

A Pathway 2 person will inadvertently and unconsciously establish a negative cycle that results in ever-increasing self-doubt as a result of acting from what I refer to as 'psychological cowardice'. For example, a young golfer deeply dreams of becoming the best golfer in the world and smashing key records, but when asked by her coach what her deepest dream is, she replies, 'To get my tour card and make a living from golf.' This response may be true, but it is not what she truly desires, so in essence it is a 'lie'. It comes from a weak or cowardly psychological place, as fear of judgement or ridicule from her coach has motivated her to understate the dream.

The following process occurs in a person's mind when they verbalise a goal from a place of psychological cowardice: the mind says to itself, 'That is not true!' and then asks itself, 'Why are you lying?' The mind then answers this question with, 'You don't think you are actually good enough to achieve it, do you?' or 'You must be embarrassed to tell them what your dream really is!'

Embarrassment is a very close relative of shame, and shame is the foundation emotion of self-doubt and fear of failure. Self-doubt and fear of failure erode enthusiasm and pollute ambition, resulting in less drive to practise or even avoidance of it. A consequence of less practice with deep focus and intent is poor skill development. Players then execute poorly more often, which in turn feeds the self-doubt and fear of failing and further reduces the motivation to practise. It is a vicious negative cycle that is incredibly hard to break.

'LA HONTE EST LA PLUS VIOLENTE DE TOUTES LES PASSIONS.'

SHAME IS THE MOST VIOLENT OF ALL THE PASSIONS.
From *La Princesse de Clèves*

Dreams do not always have to be the best in the world.

The dream does not have to be, for example, the best triathlete in the world to ignite the emotional power referred to in this section. It is absolutely fine for you to have a dream of completing Taupo's Ironman New Zealand only once, and that is all you ever do. The critical thing is that the spoken dream is true to you and your deepest, private, unspoken wish. The perception of our experience is far more important than the external reality in which we have the experience. That is, a player winning a junior club championship in golf could experience as much pleasure, joy and satisfaction as a player winning their first US Open! That is pretty neat, and makes being human so special. How we live and what we feel and experience is not limited by how much money we have or how skilled we are at something. A life lived well will make you feel like you have already achieved the dream, long before you do. When you reach this space, you are truly 'living the dream'.

In summary, Pathway 1 needs an Impossible Dream to come fully to life. Take the time to uncover your own Impossible Dream and feel your energy, focus and belief go to a new level. Treasure uncovering your dream and discussing it with your most important support people (e.g. parents, spouse or partner, or coach). It will be a pivotal moment in your life, a moment you will reflect on when you are close to achieving your dream, whatever it may be, and you will recognise that uncovering your true dream was the critical starting point for all that followed.

COMMITTING FULLY TO THE DREAM

One of the most important ingredients for you reaching your true potential is the ability to sustain a 'train-to-win' attitude and behaviour over a long period of time, often many years. Training to win involves far more than just the time spent training, however. It is about eating the right food, getting enough sleep and making life decisions that support your dream. It also involves massive attention to detail, thorough planning and developing robust and reliable habits and routines (e.g. preparation, focus and review routines). It involves reaching high levels of focus and intensity day after day, for many weeks, months and years. Commitment is perhaps the most important ingredient to reaching your potential.

Laura Langman is considered by many who know netball to be the best centre in the world, and one of the legends of the game. Her reputation is a direct result of the level of her commitment to being world class. Below is a passage from 2012 ANZ Netball

Championship winning coach Noeline Taurua, describing Laura's commitment.

THE CRITICAL INGREDIENT OF COMMITMENT IN UNCOVERING POTENTIAL

From the first time I saw Laura, at the age of 16, I always knew she would be a world-class athlete. What caught my eye was her attitude, work rate, communication skills, humour and that relentless drive of character and will. Over the years, Laura has transpired all of her innate qualities into being the best centre in the world and being the best leader that she can be. Her growth mindset will ensure that she remains that world-class athlete for many years to come.

Noeline Taurua

If you are seriously committed to becoming world class at whatever you are pursuing, then the way people describe you must reflect this. It is quite a challenge, but after reading Noeline's comments about Laura, there is no excuse, you now know what the standard is!

This level of output over such long periods of time requires a deep personal commitment throughout the journey. Consequently, one of your most important challenges is to fully invest your mind, body and spirit to each day, and to see all the little things you do as being just as important as the achievement of the final vision. Moving to a place of complete commitment, where you step across the line of no return and cut yourself off from all other possibilities, is incredibly hard, and the reason why most people never reach the goals they set in life, let alone uncover their true potential.

If there is one reason why some people succeed where others fail, it is because the successful ones are able to get themselves to do what is needed when it is needed, day after day, week after week, month after month and year after year. Make sure your mind is really clear about this. Whether you succeed in reaching your dream or not will have nothing to do with your intelligence or your bank account, but it will have everything to do with your ability to stay committed over many years, through success and failure, and adversity. Brad Kendall is another promising young New Zealand amateur golfer. The following passage of his highlights just how hard it is to get committed and remain committed to an Impossible Dream.

THE REALITY OF WHAT IT TAKES TO SUCCEED

Committing to my dream has been a lot harder than I first thought. I had been working hard, but found I was doing it for the wrong reasons. I was doing what people told me to do, but I didn't fully commit as I was only doing just enough to keep them happy, not all I could to be the best. I had a conversation with Jay (my golf

> coach) two days ago and he told me to get a job because I wasn't fully committed and wasn't making progress. This made me think about why I wasn't committing. I realised that if I was going to be successful I needed to commit fully to being world class. Training myself to commit fully to my dream is my biggest golfing challenge.
>
> **Brad Kendall**

Brad playing the third at Tauranga Golf Club

Commitment to your dream requires many steps. The following are the three most important ones:
1. getting a mentor who is world class and not family or a friend
2. paying the price and living in the 'Green Box'
3. not getting distracted.

GETTING A WORLD CLASS MENTOR

Let's say your Impossible Dream is to become the greatest golf player that has ever lived. You live in Hamilton, New Zealand and are 16 years old. Now when deciding on your mentor, ask yourself this question:

> If I could have any mentor in the world who would that be?

If you are male, then Jack Nicklaus might be the first person to put on your list.

Let's take this example a step further: imagine that you then find out where Jack lives, save money delivering papers and running an Ambrose tournament at your local club to pay for a ticket to fly to America and go and knock on his door. He opens it and says, 'Good morning.' You say, 'Good morning, Mr Nicklaus, I am _____, and I have just flown from New Zealand to ask you to be my mentor, please. I have a dream to be a great champion, just like you!'

What is Jack going to say? 'No, sorry, go away. I am reading my paper"?

He would be truly blown away that you came all the way from New Zealand just to meet him and ask. Of course he would say yes. Now, how high would your motivation, enthusiasm and hunger to practise be as you walked away after having morning tea with Jack? You would be incredibly focused. You would be unstoppable.

Here is a real-life example of what sort of psychological impact seeking out the 'impossible mentor' has on a player's practice and focus. At the time of writing this book, Luke Toomey was seeking out Rory McIlroy as a formal mentor.

CHASING RORY

The thought of asking Rory McIlroy to be my mentor was terrifying at first. I began to think of all the what-ifs, the maybes, and the devastation of facing rejection. I thought of myself as being insignificant and assumed I'd only be another 'number one fan', desperately trying to be a part of his life. However, I soon realised the reasons for which I really wanted to do it. I wanted to go where no other amateur golfer had gone. I wanted to challenge myself to live my philosophy, that being: 'I have to do what others won't to achieve what others don't.' To be the best, you need to do something that distinguishes yourself from the rest, and asking Rory over coffee to be my mentor would certainly tick that box.

As I've begun to work my way towards meeting Rory, I have injected far more focus into my training. My journey to meeting Rory has, so far, been relatively simple, and I have surprisingly got quite close very quickly. This has been a major eye-opener in terms of realising that Rory isn't too far away, and he really is just another human being. I believe with an injection of focus, passion and desire, I will meet Rory, and one day surpass him in the golfing world.

Luke Toomey

I would bet a few dozen golf balls that Luke will meet Rory in the near future and will establish a mentoring agreement with him. This will then become the greatest catalyst to Luke achieving his golfing dream. Linking in with a mentor at this level is that powerful! Sadly, for many, the thought of it is just too scary.

Now, make no mistake, attempting to connect with someone this 'important' is a massive step to get your mind to do. I have challenged so many players to do just what Luke is doing; none have! It is that challenging. Players often say to me, 'I can't just fly to America and meet Jack Nicklaus!' Why not? Underneath it all you won't because you have a deep-seated self-doubt that will whisper in your ear, 'You are not that good! Who do you think you are? Don't be so arrogant!'

This sort of 'cutting down' of ambition and belief is very common in New Zealand. If you were to say to the average New Zealander that you were going to make Jack Nicklaus your mentor, they would laugh at you! They would call you arrogant and a dreamer. However, making Jack Nicklaus your mentor is possible, and you can guarantee that if any golfer from New Zealand were to actually do it, that person would go on to be world number one. Of that I am absolutely certain. They would be a very special person.

What I hope you learn from this chapter is that massive momentum and power can come from linking in with the right mentor. I am so convinced that this is the most important ingredient for reaching any dream and uncovering potential that I make it a critical 'to do' in all my work with athletes and teams. Not all the athletes I work with access the highest possible mentor, however. Some settle for second best or someone who is local and easy to access. Some even settle for a family member or friend. I do not make it an issue, yet each time they do this, I get an uneasy feeling in my stomach that they are taking the easy road. The easy road is not Pathway 1. The easy road leads only to 'Some day I'll . . .' thinking and that route leads only to a dead end.

No matter who you look at when researching successful people in sport, business or any pursuit in life, the best all have one thing in common: they all have a 'professional' mentor. I highlighted the word professional because I see a difference between family and friends and a true 'mentor'. A family member or friend is often too soft and lets you get away with things that directly undermine your potential, simply because they do not want to upset you. A professional mentor does not care if they upset you. They have only one job: to force you to do what you say you will do by not accepting excuses, give-up talk or whining and whinging. Ideally if you went to a session with them and you had not completed your homework, they would send you away and tell you not to waste their time, even if that meant you had wasted a lot of money on air tickets or your own time.

The fastest way to learn anything in life is to spend time with the very best in whatever area you are trying to master. When I refer to a mentor, I am talking about somebody who is widely considered to be one of the best, if not the best in the world at their trade. You know whether you have picked the right person or not by simply asking yourself how you would feel asking them to be your mentor. If your answer is 'I would feel quite relaxed' then you have chosen the wrong person. The mentor must be someone who the very thought of asking and talking to actually makes you scared or nervous. When you do finally get to meet them or talk to them on the phone, your heart will be racing and your hands will be sweaty.

The Mentor's Role

The mentor's role is to make sure your plan is appropriate and that you are keeping yourself honest and doing what you said you would do. The plan includes your long-term strategic steps to success as well as your shorter-term goals, right down to your daily schedule. The mentor will maintain a careful eye over your longer-term development and growth. They must support you to make sure the right things are happening at the right time and speed, and in the right way to the right quality.

The last component of their role highlights why I do not want you to have a friend or family member as your formal mentor. There will be times when you have not followed through with what you said you would do, or your general attitude slips. It is crucial at these times that the mentor does not let you off the hook and that they challenge you. They must also challenge any excuses you make to justify why you have slipped. By making no excuses, you will feel stink. It is feeling stink that will get you back on track to doing what you said you were going to do. 'Stink' is one of the best feelings in the world for motivating you to do what is needed!

COMMITTING FULLY TO THE DREAM: EXERCISE 1

Linking in with an Inspiring Mentor

Take a few minutes to brainstorm and list down all the people you would love to have as a mentor. Do not limit yourself by 'reality' (e.g. that you live in Hamilton, New Zealand, and the person you think is critical lives in Canada). There may also be a price associated with linking in with some mentors who charge for their time. If they do, then say yes, work to save the money and pay them in cash. This will ensure you get more from the sessions because you will demand from yourself that you learn.

Ask yourself this question to help drive your thinking:

If I had no limits (e.g. money, distance, time) who would I want to mentor me?

List them here in no particular order. When you have finished, go through and rank them from first to last.

_____

_____

_____

_____

COMMITTING FULLY TO THE DREAM

Now write a shortlist of five strategies for how you would link in with the first-ranked on your list and get to meet them. For example, one may be to find out where they live, one may be to contact an agency in New Zealand to find out what links they have internationally to help set up a meeting, another may be to look at the cost of air tickets, etc.

1. _____
2. _____
3. _____
4. _____
5. _____

Now write down a few ideas about what benefits you will get from linking in with this person. For example, you will feel great motivation to train and practise, you will get detailed advice on what steps are required to be world number one, you will feel massive pride from the courage it took to meet and ask this person to be your mentor, etc.

_____
_____
_____
_____
_____
_____

Remember, the first person on your list may say no. If they do, then ask them:

> **'Who would you suggest I link in with?'**

Then you repeat the steps above and try to secure your second-choice mentor.

PAYING THE PRICE

I cannot say enough about paying the price. The term itself is incredibly powerful. It is both inspirational and brutal. 'Pay the price!' On the one hand, it tells you that all you have to do is to keep paying the price and you will be successful in achieving whatever it is that you are hunting; while on the other, it suggests that you either pay the price or you will not achieve your dream. There is no grey area when it comes to achieving your Impossible Dream; you either do or you do not! When you live from Pathway 1, you live in the REAL world, and in the real world you either fail or succeed, and that will come down to whether or not you paid the price.

In fact, if you are not prepared to pay the price to achieve your dream, you need to stop reading this book right now because it is not for you. If you do not pay the price, you will never do what is required to achieve great things (even if your dream is to win your first junior club championship in lawn bowls). You will not practise enough and, consequently, this will result in you being very unhappy with the results because your actual performance will not match up to your expectations.

Occasionally, you will see some people who look like they do not need to pay the price and seem to just go out and win, or play well without any practice or effort. Some will even tell you that if they practise too much they get worse, and have proven to themselves that practising too much is bad for them! I have found that these people are actually capable of far greater performances or reaching greater heights than they do, but due to deep, well-hidden self-doubt they do not step out and really invest or commit fully to their pursuit. They remain big fish in a little pond, whether that pond is their province, school or club. It is safer that way because they always have an excuse to fall back on: I didn't really try so I could not have expected too much.

The following story from my own life highlights how important it is to pay the price.

WHY I WAS POORER AT THIRTY-EIGHT THAN THIRTY YEARS OLD!

When I turned 30, I wrote down my financial dream. It was to be worth five million dollars by the time I was 40 years old.

When I turned 38, I stumbled across the book I had written it in. The book was covered in dust. I was poorer at 38 than I had been at 30! What became obvious to me as I dusted off the book was that my original figure was not a dream at all. It was a fantasy. At no point had I made the number a reality. There was not even a second line with my figure, let alone a plan.

When I reflected that evening on what had gone wrong, I realised that while I lived the way I did, I was never going to build that much wealth. In fact, I was not going to build any wealth.

This was how my last eight years had gone:

When my wife gave birth to our first daughter, she informed me that she wanted to go back to work. I agreed and reduced my work to be an at-home dad. Every night, when the housework was done and the little treasure was asleep, I would pour a glass of red wine, sit back and sip it, reflecting on my 'hard day's work'. I remember telling myself 'I deserved a break' and that 'I was tired and needed to rest to be ready for the next day'. I thought I had been working hard! Then, in the weekends, my wife and I worked a shift system where we had one day on and one day off, so we were able to do the things we 'wanted'. On my day off, I would go hunting, again telling myself I needed it to keep sane.

At no point in eight years had I even started to pay the price towards earning five million dollars. There was no way it was going to happen.

Now, a lot of athletes around the world make the 'I want to be world number one' statement. It is no different from my statement: 'I want to be worth five million dollars by the time I am 40.' The intention is just a fantasy. It sounds good and we say it to impress our egos and those around us!

> Until I started paying the price, I was going to be poor. And until you start paying the price, you will not reach your potential. You will remain the big fish in the little pond. However, when you are older, you will feel deep regret over all you could have achieved had you only committed and really paid the price. You will find yourself telling big stories about just how good you were when you were young, how you beat this person and that person, and how far you could have gone if you had really tried.

The Magic That Comes from Paying the Price

Once you start paying the required price to achieve your dream, something very magical happens! You start to evolve a deep sense of commitment to your dream and an even deeper belief that it will occur. This increasing belief and sense of certainty results in you paying a greater and greater price, investing more and more of what is needed (usually time), and in the end sacrificing whatever it takes. This is a common phenomenon: the more you invest in something, or the more you pay the price, the more you believe in the project itself and that it will work out in your favour, so the more you then invest. It is this powerful positive cycle that drives a person to do what they need to, hour after hour, day after day, week after week and year after year.

What Is Paying the Price?

The greatest price you will be asked to pay is time. Many people complain to me about not having enough time to fully commit to their dream. Despite this, they still spend hours watching television, going to the movies or going on vacation with friends at the expense of training, practising or performing. Many people also have too many commitments. For example, they may be trying to learn a musical instrument, play competitive sport across a number of other codes, study full-time at university and have a long-term distance relationship.

These are all really important things, but not so important that in the end they cost you your most important dream. Even your time with family and friends must often be compromised in order to train and practise at the level required to achieve the Impossible Dream. Personal pursuits outside your chosen area and activities that most other 'normal' people do in their weekends often need to be completely sacrificed for the ultimate destination, especially if your dream is large (e.g. to become the best extreme skier in the world). Once you fully commit to a dream that big you are no longer part of the 'normal' group. You have automatically joined a very abnormal group in which the rules are different. You have to start to watch what you eat and drink, what you do with your time, how much sleep and rest you get, etc.

Many athletes also complain about being unbalanced. If they have a dream of being the best in the world, or even one of the best in their province, then there will be a related cost that they must pay. They need to accept that their life will be unbalanced when compared to 'normal' people their age. Then there is the actual financial cost associated with achieving their dream. The time needed to earn that money cuts further into other 'normal' activities (e.g. movies with friends, sleeping in at the weekends, etc).

Family and Paying the Price

Family is a point worthy of its own section. When talking with athletes about family and paying the price, I emphasise that, in general, family must come first! This sounds like a contradiction to the above passages, but it is not. It is possible for an athlete to put family first, and also ensure they are able to commit the time needed for their dream every day.

To genuinely put your family first, you should sit with them and identify key family commitments for the year that need to be on the calendar. You should then do your utmost to plan the year around those dates. What usually happens when having these discussions with family is that they tell you to put your pursuit first, especially if an important event clashes with a family occasion. I've found that athletes who are able to sit with their families and have these discussions are often those who are the least selfish. They will also be the ones who, when it comes to the crunch and they have to decide between their pursuit and their family, always put their family first; even if, for example, that means walking off the last round of a massive event to be with family during a crisis.

Athletes like this are settled and stable individuals. They don't have to prove anything to anybody, and just love doing what they do. They have strong relationships with their loved ones because they are genuinely more important to them than anything else. Ironically, this results in them performing better because they have pure minds and do not need the outcome to feel complete.

In summary, no matter how you plan out your career, there is no way you can achieve your end point without frequently and repeatedly paying the price. It is not a one-off payment that covers you for long periods of time, nor is it possible to pay a massive amount one week (e.g. 60 hours practice) and then only a minimal amount the next (e.g. 4 hours practice). You need to keep paying the required price day after day, week after week and year after year if you are ever going to uncover your true potential and achieve an Impossible Dream.

PAYING THE PRICE SPEAKS FOR ITSELF!

New Zealand rowers are among the best in the world. They are regular winners at World Championships and excel at Olympic Games. That is because of one thing: they pay an enormous price! Rowers are widely known within the elite sporting community, along with multiathletes (e.g. triathletes and ironpeople), for setting the benchmark for work ethic. It is because of this that I often recommend that rugby players I work with who are looking for a flat move in with a rower, as this will help them see what paying the price really looks like.

Launching jetties at the Rowing New Zealand High Performance Centre at Lake Karāpiro in Cambridge. This is the place to be in New Zealand if you are ever going to make it on the world stage in rowing!

COMMITTING FULLY TO THE DREAM: EXERCISE 2

Paying the Price

The easiest way to see if you are paying the required price to achieve your Impossible Dream is to look at your weekly schedule. Answering this question will instantly let you know if you are!

How many hours last week did I spend doing X?

X is practising or training in your pursuit (e.g. in rugby it is catch pass, in golf it is hitting the ball). Do not include performance minutes (e.g. time playing rounds of golf in competition or a game of rugby). Write only hours practising or training.

Write the number here: _____

Write your Impossible Dream here:

_____
_____
_____
_____

Now look at the number of hours and read your dream to yourself. Note down what is going through your mind right now:

_____
_____
_____
_____
_____
_____
_____

If the hours do not match the dream it is likely you are thinking quite strong thoughts about how the dream is not going to happen if you keep that pattern up.

Sometimes, though, people do not know what paying the price actually looks like! This is due to them never looking outside their immediate surroundings and thinking that all people around the world are just like their little group in little New Zealand.

To see what paying the price to reach your potential and achieve your dream really looks like, have a look online at the following YouTube clips:

http://www.youtube.com/watch?v=knIlrbozmts
http://www.youtube.com/watch?v=aNwnPEIsJGE
http://www.youtube.com/watch?v=yZ63p1UFLGE

The last URL takes you to a series of clips on NZ SAS training. Take your time when watching the SAS clips as there many gold nuggets in there that will help inspire you and show you if you are truly paying the price. Enjoy!

Now write a few notes to yourself. Are you paying the price required? If not, why not, and what needs to change to get yourself to start paying the price and keep paying the price? If you are already paying the price, give yourself a pat on the back and then get back to work.

_____
_____
_____
_____
_____
_____
_____
_____

The Green Box

It is critical to understand that paying the price is more than just spending time doing something. It is also about how you do what it is you do. When somebody fully pays the price, they spend the right amount of time doing the right things in the right way, and at the correct level of focus and intensity. This is what I call 'living in the Green Box'! Here is a great example of how it is possible to think and believe you are doing enough, when you are really just going through the motions. This passage is from one of New Zealand's top up-and-coming young professional golfers, Nick Gillespie.

> ### ARE YOU REALLY PAYING THE PRICE OR JUST GOING THROUGH THE MOTIONS?
>
> There is no better feeling than turning up to an event knowing you have done everything to give yourself the best possible chance of performing at your best. For a while I thought what I was doing was giving me this each week, but realistically I was living in a 'bullsh*t world' – a made-up front to make me feel better about my 45 hours of 'golf' a week. When I actually sat down and recorded my practise and training, it quickly became apparent that I wasn't putting in enough quality time and my approach was not up to PGA standard.
>
> If you want to compete with those guys, you have to surpass their workload. I had to take a good look at myself and really be honest. Sure, I was spending a lot of time at the golf course, but I was not working smart. Through working with DG and the team around me over the last few months, I am able to say now that I'm starting to live in the real world, although I still have a way to go to get my practice schedule and approach to an event where they should be. And guess what – my results have now started to trend in the right direction too! No coincidence there.
>
> **Nick Gillespie**

When I was a young boy, my father was a farm shepherd. I remember him earning 25 dollars a week. Every six weeks we would drive 60 miles on a shingle road in the Vauxhall Viva to get groceries in town. I remember that on those trips, if the weather was nice, Mum and Dad would buy us fish and chips for tea, and we would eat them on the beach. If we were really lucky, we were allowed tomato sauce! Growing up, my parents ingrained simple but powerful life messages in me without having to say a word: 'Appreciate the little things', 'Nothing worthwhile comes easy' and

'If you want to achieve anything in life you have to earn it through hard work!'

I have been a psychologist for 13 years. In that time, their life lessons have been reinforced so often that in my mind they have become powerful immutable laws. What we put in we get out! If we do not pay the price we achieve nothing of any worth.

Perhaps more importantly, these life lessons have taught me that success has nothing to do with talent, intelligence or your bank account. It has everything to do with the number of minutes you commit to whatever it is you do. Commit enough minutes with a good plan and good mentoring or coaching and you will be successful!

In my first year working with the Chiefs in 2009 we made the Super Rugby Final. In 2010 we were struggling to win games. Towards the end of the campaign we were sitting 10th on the table. One day, when I was watching the team train, I thought I would test my 'law' and see if the lads were actually paying the price required to win and succeed.

I used the following grid to help my little experiment. It is a grid I had used many times in my work with clients with depression who would come to me complaining that they were a failure and their lives would never result in anything worthwhile. I would simply get them to rate their habits and behaviours on the grid. It was always very powerful for them to see that the reason they were failing was because they never did enough to warrant success – because they lived in the red. The grid did not need all the descriptions provided. I found that simply the first row of words were enough for the client to understand exactly what I was saying. These are: **'Never Does Enough'**, **'Does Just Enough'** and **'Always Does Extra'**.

NEVER DOES ENOUGH	DOES JUST ENOUGH (going through the motions)	ALWAYS DOES EXTRA
Has days each week without practising core skills at all	Practises core skills just during scheduled team times	Practises core skills every day
Arrives late often and is usually last to arrive, but always first to leave	Arrives on time, but never early; not first to leave but never last to leave	Arrives an hour before training starts to do stretches and bands
Contributes nothing at analysis sessions or on park when questions asked	Contributes sometimes	Is usually very warm and even sweating when coach is ready to start
Never leads anything in drills or exercises	Does enough homework not to look silly	If coach is late, starts anyway
Never cleans up after self or others	Sleeps in if gets the chance	Hates it when training cancelled
Complains about things behind people's backs	Happy when sessions cancelled or delayed	Always contributes; runs things; does more homework than is expected
Never helps others; enjoys seeing others struggle and fail	Waits for coach and trainers to start session	Helps others even at cost to self
Puts others down for being in 'green'	Helps others when directed to do so (e.g. coach has asked them), and usually only when there is something to gain	Always eats right and controls alcohol consumption – or does not drink at all
Indulges in frequent excessive eating and drinking	Indulges in occasional excessive eating and drinking	Skin fold test results excellent
Skin fold test results terrible	Skin fold test results ok	

Continuing the story about the Chiefs in 2010 – once I had drawn up the grid I went through and made a tally mark for each player based on how I had seen their habits during that campaign. There were approximately 35 players at training that day. There were six in green and five each in red and yellow. The rest were on the border between yellow and red. Only six in green! Twenty-nine players in yellow or lower, and twenty-four in red/yellow or red! When I lined up the grid with the competition table and called the far right (green) edge first and the bottom right (red) edge last, the line between red and yellow was about 10th and 11th and that is where we were on the table! We were 10th not because we were useless and had poor players, we were 10th based on poor habits.

In 2012 and 2013 the Chiefs won back-to-back Super 15 Rugby titles. This was a direct result of the senior players living in the GREEN and demanding that the team live here too!

In 2012 and 2013 the Chiefs won back-to-back Championships. Throughout both campaigns, there were multiple players living in the green, while most lived on the border of yellow and green and only three or four were in the red. The ones in the red did not gain selection. Again, this reinforced the messages my parents had taught me when I was a boy, and what I had seen so many times across my career as a psychologist: pay the price, live in the green and you will be successful! This is critical for developing a powerful performance mindset and mental fitness. Consistently living in the Green Box will help you to grow mentally fit and tough, to pay the price and not get distracted when other things come along.

It is no surprise that Richard Kahui and Stephen Donald were in the Rugby World Cup final considering how fully they lived in the Green Box doing their day-to-day 'work' conditioning, rehabbing their bodies, doing game analysis and training their core skills.

COMMITTING FULLY TO THE DREAM

The power of living in the green is as massive for individuals as it is for a team, no matter what area of life we are talking about: sport, school, business . . . in fact, anything you do! If you have not made it, or things are not working out, it is likely because you are not living in the green.

COMMITTING FULLY TO THE DREAM: EXERCISE 3

What Box Are You Living In?

Now you understand what is meant by red, yellow and green boxes, decide which one you have been living in until now.

Then sit down with your coach, parents or partner and ask them which box they think you have been living in.

NEVER DOES ENOUGH	DOES JUST ENOUGH	ALWAYS DOES EXTRA

Write a few comments to yourself based on your thoughts and the feedback from others. Are you happy with the box you are living in? If so, why? If you are unhappy with your habits and the box you are living in, and think you will not reach your dream staying in this box, give yourself a few short messages and suggestions about what needs to change. Feel free to speak strongly to yourself.

Building Your Own Green Box

Building your own Green Box is easy. It does not require you to come up with complicated and difficult things that you have to do. The Green Box needs to be built around very simple actions that are completely within your control (e.g. how early you arrive before a lesson, what you eat for breakfast, how long you practise for each day, etc). The key point is that the behaviours in the Green Box are ones you can follow every day and are directly linked to success!

Here is my own Green Box. I have high cholesterol and a terrible family history of death due to massive heart attacks. Hence, for me, remaining fit and eating well are directly linked to success – staying alive! That is what I mean by directly linked to success. If you did not do one of these behaviours repeatedly over a long period of time, it would cost you your dream and, likewise, if you did do it, it would be directly linked to your subsequent success.

MY GREEN BOX

1. Run or do another form of exercise every day.
2. Eat porridge with raisins and banana or organic poached eggs on homemade toast for breakfast.
3. Review plan for the day – written down the night before.
4. Wash the dishes after breakfast and then every night before bed.
5. Write something in my sports psychology book.
6. Intentionally fail at something without anyone knowing.
7. Have daily relaxation sessions.

Note: This list is not driven by obsessive compulsion making me feel that if I did not follow it my world would fall apart! I do these things because of the great way they make me feel. They put me on the front foot every day and I feel alive! When I do these things it results in me operating from my potential and being very effective.

Doing these things provides fuel or momentum to live my Pathway 1 philosophy!

COMMITTING FULLY TO THE DREAM: EXERCISE 4
Building Your Green Box

Now it is time for you to build your own Green Box behaviours. List them below. There should be more than five but less than 10 or 11 behaviours that you can make happen every day. Try to relate them directly to your sport or pursuit, so you won't have to 'find' time if you are already very busy (e.g. you may have stretching as a daily Green Box behaviour because you know you need to stretch).

1. _____
2. _____
3. _____
4. _____
5. _____

When you are happy with your behaviours, go and show them to your coach, parents or partner. Make sure you then put them somewhere public, such as on the fridge, to remind you and others what you are committing to do.

NOT GETTING DISTRACTED

I was fascinated to learn that the word 'decide' comes from a root word that means 'to cut off from'. This is a splendid way to describe the third crucial component for achieving full commitment to the Impossible Dream. It is exactly what needs to occur if you are ever going to reach your potential. For you to deeply and fully decide to pursue a dream, you have to cut yourself off from all other distractions or possibilities.

If you maintain other links and connections in case you fail in your main pursuit, you will ironically increase the very chance that you will ultimately fail. Being in two or more minds is the greatest danger to any dream. Great dreams are not achieved by many people. This is because most people can't fully cut themselves off from having options B and C just in case A does not work out. As a result of the mind holding on to multiple options, a pure state of mind is never reached and pure Pathway 1 courage and absolute commitment is never obtained.

Cutting off from all other distractions is an absolute must, no matter what your life dream, and this is even more so when it comes to really big dreams (e.g. becoming the world's best golfer). There are probably millions of other players who dream of becoming world number one. Almost all of them will not make it! I know that this is blunt, but this discussion is about living in the real world of what it takes to be successful; not living in what I refer to as the 'bullsh*t world'. It is from a 'real world' discussion with yourself that you will actually see if your dream is really what you say it is. If your dream is truly your dream then when thinking about the price you must pay to achieve it your mind will tell you, 'I will do whatever it takes and pay whatever the cost to achieve my dream!'

When I have the 'paying the price' discussion with athletes, many uncover that they do not actually want to be the best in the world or even in their province. This is great because they find out that what they thought was their deepest dream was not their dream at all. Our work then focuses on uncovering what their Impossible Dream actually is. I am always pleased when my clients end up reaching a place of 'truth' during these discussions. If you are not completely truthful with yourself, your coach and/or your family about how a dream may not actually be 'the dream', you and they could spend the next 10 to 15 years investing in a 'failing business'. In the end, it would lead only to tears, regret, unhappiness and a lot of wasted funds. What would be most sad, however, is that you would not have connected with your true dream and would have missed out on time that could have been spent living from a pure mind and spirit.

COMMITTING FULLY TO THE DREAM: EXERCISE 5

Identifying Current and Potential Distractions That Threaten to Blow Up Your Dream

List any current distractions in your life (e.g. lots of advice to do full-time university study; partner wants more time with you; urged to take on more work to have more money in the bank just in case you fail; family issues; procrastination; the weather where you live, etc).

Go through the list and rank the distractions in order from those having the most impact on your time and dream to those having the least impact. Also rank them based on how much control you have over each one. For example, you may have chosen to play three sports, each one requiring an equal amount of time every week to practise and play. No one is making you play all three and you have complete control over which ones you continue with.

Now scribble an action or solution next to each distraction. For example, in the situation of playing too many sports you may decide to withdraw from two and focus on one. Then act: phone your coaches right away and talk to them. If talking on the phone is just too hard, send emails asking to meet them so you can talk about your need to withdraw. Do not wait.

Using Self-talk to Remain Disciplined

When you notice your mind starting to get off track (e.g. wanting to spend more time surfing when you are working hard and feel you deserve a break; wanting to take up another hobby or sport, etc) think the following:

I WILL NOT get distracted!

I WILL pay the price!

I WILL be disciplined!

After saying these messages to yourself, it is important you have actions to go and 'do'. Your Green Box serves as an anchor to go to when you are on the edge of being distracted. For example, I have cleaning the dishes on my Green Box list. When I find myself wanting to go to bed without doing the dishes, or watch a movie after dinner instead, I simply say to myself, 'I will not get distracted' and 'I will pay the price', and I go and do the dishes. Then I praise myself: 'Good man, David!' This increases my self-pride and injects deeper motivation to hold to my dream plan. It feels really good. And on I go.

Growing Mental Fitness and Toughness Through the Patience Mind Gym

Many athletes, and people in general for that matter, struggle to live in the Green Box and find it almost impossible not to give in to distractions. They seem to function well for a certain period of time, sometimes even for months, and then all of a sudden just fall off track. When talking to them about their slip they often say that they did not have the mental toughness not to get distracted: 'It is just too hard!'

What they are actually saying is that they were not mentally fit enough to stick to their daily Green Box behaviour, and they got mentally tired or fatigued and resorted back to old habits. Some people don't even last months; a week or even a day is their limit! Sound familiar? More than likely. The theme I hear most when talking with athletes is their wanting to have better mental discipline and focus.

Finding a way to grow mental focus, toughness and fitness is something I have given a lot of thought to. As a result of ongoing experimentation with names and ideas, the 'patience mind gym' evolved. Quite simply, the patience mind gym is finding any behaviour that takes time and discipline to do slowly and deliberately, and then continuing to do it until the task is completed (or a block of the work is completed if the task is too big to finish in one session, e.g. weeding the garden or painting the house). There are many tasks and exercises that fit this description.

One great patience mind gym example from my own experience is moving bricks.

MOVING BRICKS

Over the years of living in our home, we gradually lifted up all the old slippery bricks from the various paths throughout the garden and put them in one massive pile. In the end, there were around 2000 bricks in one pile. I walked past this pile one day and

realised that it would be an excellent mind gym exercise to move those bricks, one brick at a time, and stack them behind the shed!

I started piling each one into the wheelbarrow, but after only three bricks, my mind wandered, and I said to myself, 'I am bored!'

What that told me was that my mental fitness or toughness was only three bricks long! And I was a sports psychologist! So, at every second or third brick, I said to myself, 'I will be patient and I will be thorough.' I noticed my mind start to focus and settle. It took 14 hours to move all the bricks! This picture was taken halfway through to completion.

I look for different mind gyms to keep extending my mental fitness all the time now. I have just finished cutting the winter supply of firewood and, when tidying up the branches, I allowed myself to move only one branch at a time!

Another mind gym I do on a daily basis is washing the dishes. We do not have a dishwasher, and we never will! Doing the dishes every night before bed has had a massive impact on my mental fitness. Many times my mind has tried to persuade me that I can do the dishes in the morning and it will not matter, or that I deserve a night off as I have been working hard and need a break, or that we deserve a dishwasher!

DOING THE DISHES

A familiar sight at the end of my every day – dishes that need doing before bed. At 10.30 at night, sometimes later, it takes a lot of 'I will be patient' and 'I will be thorough' to finish the dishes properly, I assure you!

On average, it takes me one and a half hours a day to do the morning and evening dishes. That is one and a half hours of patience mind gym every day!

The other day, as I got close to finishing this book, I noticed a deep feeling of unease. I wanted to rush and get it finished as soon as possible; I just could not wait. I was deeply excited with how it was turning out and I wanted it done, now! With that in mind I took myself to the mind gym for a booster mind workout and made myself do the dishes extra slowly. It took me over one and a half hours to do the evening dishes; I started at 8.30 p.m. and finished just after 10 p.m. It worked a treat!

The hardest challenge comes when I have done the dishes and

> am heading off to bed, only to find a coffee cup or plate tucked away somewhere where my wife or daughters were having a drink or snack during the day. I pick up the item, head back to the sink and wash it.
>
> At first, my mind tried all sorts of ways to get out of doing the dishes, but over time I have grown to really enjoy the challenge.

As a result of 18 months doing the dishes every day and utilising opportunities such as moving those bricks, I have found my mind growing in mental toughness all the time. This is most obvious at times when I have needed to finish off a project or job of some type. In the past I would have procrastinated, and in most circumstances left jobs half-finished. Not any more! My mind notices the old urge to delay and procrastinate, and smashes it with key phrases such as: 'Work before play, Galbraith', 'Don't get distracted', 'Finish off the job', 'I will pay the price', 'I will be patient' and 'I will be thorough!' The most common phrase I use to remind myself to finish jobs off though is 'DO YOUR DISHES!' I cannot adequately put into words the huge impact this simple concept has had on my life.

POSSIBLE PATIENCE MIND GYM EXERCISES

- Knitting: get yourself to knit 50 lines every day, slowly and carefully, with high attention to detail.

- Doing the dishes: do the dishes by hand every night before bed.

- Weeding the garden: first outline the area to be weeded and work until you complete the designated area, weed by weed. Continue section by section.

- Stacking bricks: buy 50 bricks and move them, one by one, from one place in the yard to another, again working slowly and deliberately with focus and concentration.

- Shifting marbles: take one marble at a time from a jar, swap it from one hand to the other and placing it in another jar carefully and quietly, again with focus and concentration.

- Doing a jigsaw: buy yourself a 5000-piece jigsaw puzzle that will take many days, weeks or months to complete. Do 10 to 20 pieces every day. To really make this a powerful mind gym exercise, choose a theme that does not interest you in the slightest (e.g. if you are a young man, buy a princess puzzle!). This will build very powerful mental toughness due to the immense discipline required to do it.

- Painting the house: this is similar to the weeding example. Painting the house will take a long time if done properly. Designate the area to be attacked and get started, preparing first, then painting, again with high attention to detail and the quality of the job. Move on only when one particular area is completed. This may even be done one board at a time!

- Tipping matchsticks: this is similar to the marbles exercise. Tip matchsticks out of a box and then restack them.

- Performing daily stretching exercises or relaxation drills.

During your mind gym, expect that your mind will get bored and want to give up or will get distracted with something else it thinks is more important, more fun or easier! This is supposed to happen; that is why there is nothing fun on the patience mind gym list. It is supposed to be mind numbing and deeply boring.

As the mind starts to get bored, impatient and/or distracted, simply use the appropriate phrase from the list below and gently roll it over in your head. You will find that using the right phrase simply nullifies the urge to give up, rush or do something else. In time, following this process will build powerful, deep anchors in your unconscious mind that 'fire' each time you find yourself getting impatient, distracted or wanting to give up. The unconscious mind will link immediately to the phrases you have been using during your mind gym and this will in turn generate a deep, quiet urge to push through and hang in doing what is needed to finish the job off.

I will be patient!

I will be thorough!

I will finish the job off!

Just relax! (You can use deep breathing with this one)

Linking the Patience Mind Gym to Your Sport

You can immediately start using whichever phrase you like from those above, or one of your own, when practising, training and performing. They are especially useful in any circumstances when you begin to feel desperate to perform better or to hurry up and finish a good performance before the wheels fall off!

For example, you are playing golf and are three under your handicap after 13 holes. You notice your mind start to get tense, and whisper to yourself, 'I hope this round finishes soon, before the wheels fall off.'

It is now that you would use your little phrase you had been practising during your mind gym to help yourself have patience and discipline:

I will be patient!

I will be thorough!

I will stick to my routine, shot by shot!

You do not just have to use it when you are starting to get impatient or desperate. You can use it as a part of your normal performance routines to help build and maintain a deep patience, calm and thoroughness.

The following passage is by a great friend and colleague of mine,

Reon Sayer. Reon is a qualified AAA PGA professional golf coach and a senior coach at the St Peter's Golf Academy at St Peter's School in Cambridge, New Zealand. He was a successful New Zealand amateur golfer who then played professional golf on the PGA Tour of Australasia. Reon represented New Zealand 21 times. When he told me how the patience mind gym had helped him be a great dad, I knew his story just had to be included.

A REAL LIFE EXAMPLE OF HOW THE PATIENCE MIND GYM CAN HAVE A MASSIVE IMPACT ON SOMEONE'S LIFE!

Within my current coach and management roles here at the St Peter's Golf Academy and New Zealand Golf, I have been lucky enough to work with and learn from David Galbraith for many years. We share the belief that good people will always outlast great sportspeople; combine the two and you may just end up with someone very special that has a realistic chance of being world number one.

Sports at a high level can be an extremely lonely and at times selfish place. Weaknesses can show very quickly when pressure is applied. Impatience was a negative quality within my character, which hurt me many times when trying to achieve, and it's for that reason that I am continually trying to improve myself to better equip players I work with.

I set out on this mind gym exercise to help continue to improve my patience.

The Fence

In early 2013, with the pending arrival of our first born, and after some frank and honest conversations with work colleagues about the life changes I was about to go through, it hit home that I had some tough challenges ahead, above all else being a good father and husband with very limited sleep. I'd always felt I needed eight to nine hours of sleep each night to operate properly, which even with a well-settled baby wasn't going to happen, especially early on. Combine this with a lifestyle of one who had always come and gone as he pleased, and I could feel the break being applied a little more each day as we got closer to the due date. I could already feel the impatience building, and not for the reason it should have been – wanting the due date to hurry along. It was impatience combined with that other awful character trait, selfishness, that my comfortable lifestyle was very much in for change.

I had undertaken patience mind gym exercises before, my favourite being trimming the lawn edges with scissors. I did this not so much for the mind gym exercise in itself, but for the entertainment value of the reaction of passers-by, thinking they lived next to a crazy. Crazy, no; obsessive, yes. When you are wired to the right mindset of doing your best at everything you try, you must be obsessed to be eventually great at it. I have great lawn edges, and I also have a brand-new petrol line trimmer. Time now saved in the garden means more time to be a good dad. I don't miss the scissors, but it was a simple weekly exercise that started me on the right track.

My latest exercise was painting my fence. This was 120 metres if both sides are taken into consideration, and was a combination of palings and trellis. It was a big job, but I still had the luxury of time – roughly 45 hours of painting over three months in the end. No radio, no Wi-Fi, just time to think. Absolutely there would have been easier ways to do it, as at least eight passers-by told me, but there would have been no challenge in it, and in no way would it have helped my impatience. Spraying it would have been obvious, which it was, but the point of the whole exercise would have been missed. Each one of those people that passed by and took the time to chat would have left me thinking, 'Crazy!' One asked, 'What are you doing?' to which I replied, 'Painting my fence.' Nothing else was said as he walked away, shaking his head. Self-acceptance is one of the great keys to unlocking the enjoyment of life. I now have a great-looking fence.

The fence!

Florence Isabelle Sayer arrived in March and, now being December, I can reflect on the first eight months of her life – extremely rewarding, challenging and tiring all in the same sentence. Florence suffered from gastro-oesophageal reflux during the early months of her life and, having experienced it, I wouldn't wish it on anyone, especially mum and baby. But, as a loving family, we coped. Improved patience meant that, even during those tough times, often at 2 a.m., holding her after three hours of continuous screaming, I still felt I had control of the situation, and she is now a bonnie child without a care in the world. If you want any information on reflux go to: www.reflux.org.au

Through patience mind gym exercises, I have learnt that life brings choices and those choices bring challenges – challenges that may be good or bad – but it's not until one has time to reflect on those challenges that they can take full responsibility for their choices. For me, choices now bring opportunities to improve Me.

Reon Sayer

COMMITTING FULLY TO THE DREAM: EXERCISE 6
Building Your Own Patience Mind Gym

Take a few minutes now to think about what patience mind gym you can start today. Do not wait until tomorrow to start. Do it right now! My patience mind gym will be:

_____

_____

_____

Remember to write your mind gym in your Green Box! If you really want to grow mental discipline, do two sets per day – one when you wake up and one before bed.

I have found now, after doing the dishes every night for 18 months, it actually makes me feel inspired, the same as if I have been for a run! I feel clearheaded, energised and on the front foot. That is how your mind gym will make you feel if you settle on the right one and keep doing it.

In summary, when you fully commit to the Impossible Dream and cut yourself off from all other possibilities, something very special happens in your mind. You enter a world where you feel deeply content, peaceful and at one with the universe. This is the opposite of what most people think would occur from committing to just one thing. Most people believe that they would feel vulnerable and as if they have got everything to lose. Ironically, this only happens if you live from cowardice, or from Pathway 2 – the pathway of self-doubt and fear of failure – and do not focus on the Impossible Dream.

Living from Pathway 1 – committing to the pathway of courage and uncovering an Impossible Dream – gives you a powerful mindset. Each of the processes discussed in this chapter – (1)

linking in with a mentor, (2) paying the price and living in the Green Box, and (3) growing mental fitness and patience through the mind gym – all help you develop a pure mindset, resulting in your mind letting go of fear of failure and desperation to achieve the end point.

It is the 'letting go' of fear of failure that allows you to sustain a train-to-win attitude and behaviour over a long period of time – often years because nothing you do is 'obsessively' driven or forced! It is when you start to force yourself to do things to avoid failing that you start to get worn out and tired, because you never feel like you have actually done enough to succeed!

If you can tick off the steps covered so far in this book you will have established a blueprint for operating from passion. That is why, at this point, I expect you to start falling in love with your pursuit and really wanting to practise. It is an incredible power to be unleashing on the world!

QUICK REVIEW EXERCISE

Write down here the five most important things you have learnt from reading this book so far that will help you uncover your potential in sport and life:

1. _____

2. _____

3. _____

4. _____

5. _____

_____

Now go and share these five things with your partner, parents and/or coach. Make sure you tell them how these five things are now going to happen and how they will help your pursuit and your life!

DEVELOPING THE STRATEGIC PLAN TO SUCCESS

A key indicator of your commitment to the Impossible Dream will be the level of detail you have in your planning, both short- and long-term. The more detail you have in your 'Strategic Plan to Success', the greater will be the underlying commitment to it in your heart and soul. Often people tell me they are committed to changing their life or achieving a great goal or wonderful dream, but when I ask them to tell or show me the plan, there is a long silence. This silence tells me that their end point is really just a fantasy and not a goal or dream at all. Any destination without a plan is just a fantasy!

The depth of detail in your planning will indicate the likelihood of you achieving your dream. Ironically, achieving your dream will never be in doubt when you have a detailed plan, have a deep

Pathway 1 philosophy of courage, live in the Green Box and live by the core values of patience and family. Doing what is required today, over many weeks, months and years, will result in your dream being realised. By the time you reach it, it will be of no surprise at all that you have done so, as you will have spent the right amount of time doing the right thing in the right way. Your repeated habits, successes and failures will eventually lead you to the desired outcome.

If any one word has stood out over the years in this job when I've described those athletes and people who have made it compared to those who have not it would be 'clarity'. Getting clarity comes from having a detailed plan! Here is a brief comment about the importance of planning from Matt Perry, one of New Zealand's most exciting young golfing prospects. Matt won the 2011 New Zealand amateur title and represented the New Zealand Eisenhower team in 2012.

GET REAL ABOUT PLANNING!

I quickly learnt the value of planning towards my Impossible Dream. To achieve anything worth achieving you MUST live in the REAL world. That basically means no excuses, no bullsh*t. YOU either do the work, or you don't – simple.

Planning is a huge part of reaching goals and stepping closer to achieving the Impossible Dream. I have always planned. But I've recently become a lot clearer on planning and goal setting and have taken it to a new level, stipulating exactly what I want to achieve each time I do work. This has made a huge difference and I've seen my 'process' improve dramatically. It was no surprise to see that my recent 2013 'outcomes' have followed suit.

I plan everything using daily, weekly, monthly, yearly and 15-year plans. It is the only way I can see a clear pathway to my Impossible Dream. Without planning, it would become a 'what could have been' rather than an Impossible Dream.

Matt playing in China in 2014.

Matt Perry

LIONS AND LAMBS

Athletes who have clarity stand out from the rest like lions from lambs. Everything about them is fundamentally different. They have vigour in the way they walk and talk. They always put the right effort in the right place for the right amount of time, doing the right things. The phrase on their tombstone might read:

NO WASTED MINUTES!

They make a pretty special specimen. Coaches and psychologists get very excited when they encounter such an athlete, as they know that they will uncover their potential and likely go a very long way. They are the gold nuggets you do not stumble across very often, but when you do, your heart jumps.

The most exciting thing is, planning is something you have complete control over. You are not born a great or poor planner; there is no DNA or genetic structures that cause us to be one way or another. There are certain things that must happen for you to plan well. This next section will cover these so you can do them yourself.

DEVELOPING THE STRATEGIC PLAN TO SUCCESS: EXERCISE 1

Identify How Much Clarity You Have Right Now!

There are some critical areas where world-class gold-medal quality athletes have crystal-clear clarity. As you read through this list, rate yourself against each point, with 10 being exactly like you (e.g. 10 for number one means that you are very clear about what the end point will look like).

It will be interesting to see just how good at planning you already are.

1. They are very clear about what the end product or end point will look like (have video footage, still pictures and book of each part of 'their game').

2. They are very clear about how good they are at their core skills. They live in the real world not the bullsh*t world by testing and getting objective feedback through stats.

3. They are very clear about how long-term targets can be broken down into workable chunks or periods, so they do not try to do anything they are not yet ready to move on to. They are very good at doing step A first, then step B, etc, in the right order and at the right time.

4. They are very clear about what their weekly schedule looks and what their daily objectives are.

5. Finally, they are very clear about what they are doing right now

and why (i.e. why they are hitting this shot in this way or doing this particular drill). They live by the law 'Always do something for a reason'.

Add your score out of 50.

Clarity score: _____ /50

Write a few notes to yourself about how clear you are right now. Are you clear about where you are trying to end up and what you need to do to get there? Give yourself praise where it is deserved and, if required, be hard on yourself to get greater clarity!

WHY CLARITY IS SO IMPORTANT

Athletes who score high on clarity do not get ahead of themselves and try to achieve outcomes ahead of time. They do not get caught up wondering what they could have or should have done differently in the past. They do not feel desperate that time is running out or petrified that the wheels will fall off, or that they are going to fail. They live firmly rooted in today and have fierce patience for tomorrow. They have deep trust that tomorrow will take care of itself as long as they take care of what needs to be done today.

These athletes stick to what is on their plan, doing the right thing at the right time, the right way, for however long is required. They do not think about outcome, their last result or how they will perform tomorrow. They do not get stuck wondering why they keep making mistakes when they practise, instead focusing on injecting Pathway 1 courage into their routine, trying to achieve a pure performance zone and learning from today to be better tomorrow.

Not surprisingly, these athletes also perform moment-by-moment, living fully in the here and now. The following section will step you through each of the points above so you can establish them for yourself.

> ### 'CLARITY AFFORDS FOCUS.'
> THOMAS LEONARD

HAVING CLARITY ABOUT WHAT THE END PRODUCT WILL LOOK LIKE

There is a lovely story in Dan Coyle's book *Talent Code* that highlights this point perfectly. It is about an eight-year-old tennis player who was ranked number one in the United States for her age. The interesting thing about this young up-and-coming player was that she hit the tennis ball like Roger Federer, especially her backhand. When Dan Coyle visited her family's home, he found a large television in the lounge surrounded by videos of Roger Federer's games. All the family loved Federer and watched most of his matches. Further, the eight year old had spent hours and hours of her life watching him play, and then set about mastering how he played the game. She had mirrored his backhand to a point where she hit it frame-for-frame like he did. In essence, she had evolved an unconscious (and conscious) blueprint for how to hit a backhand and then had proceeded to follow this until her own backhand matched the picture. My belief is that it was the power of the unconscious blueprint that had subsequently led to this eight-year-old hitting the ball like Federer.

The lesson for all of us here is that the clearer the conscious and unconscious representation of the desired end point, the harder the mind works to get you there. It is as though an unseen energy or force propels or pulls you across time and space to achieve what the mind most desperately desires. A great metaphor would be to picture a large rubber band or piece of elastic between the here and now and the final destination; the thicker and stronger the band (i.e. the greater the clarity about the end point) the greater the force pulling you towards the final destination.

Imagination test!
Imagine a large thick rubber band pulled tightly between your fingers, and then imagine the force as the band tries to pull your fingers together . . .

It is critical that you visualise the end point as vividly as possible. This should involve a clear representation of the final 'whole' product, and a breakdown of the key steps, or what I refer to as the A, B, Cs of what you will do to get there. Technology in sport is so advanced now that it is easy to generate vivid, and even three-dimensional, representations of what the end point will look like in frame-by-frame, high-definition clarity. It is also possible to superimpose representations of yourself into your images. It is an exciting way to generate a powerful image bank for your mind to absorb and hold as your true north, or where you are going!

DEVELOPING THE STRATEGIC PLAN TO SUCCESS: EXERCISE 2

Building Clarity About What the End Point Will Look Like

Sit down with your coach and discuss what you will look like when you reach your dream. Build visual clarity by looking at others around the world who do what you do. Find YouTube clips, photos and anything that helps you build a vivid picture.

Make sure you build a picture of all elements of what you do. For example, in golf you would include a representation for each key element of the game (i.e. the drive, the long iron, the short irons, the wedges and sand iron, and putting). Watch these clips often, ideally just before you practise. Imagine what it would be like to load them onto an iPad to take in your training bag, and watch them before you practise and during your breaks.

As you master relaxation (covered shortly) you can relax while watching these clips. This will open your unconscious mind to all the images, virtually burning them into your mind as the target or end point that the mind will now seek.

You should find that this exercise generates a thrill of excitement as you connect with what you will look like when you get to your end point. This excitement should give you the motivation to practise and perform right now. Your will be motivated from deep passion, not an obsessive-compulsive drive, and you will feel deep sadness every time you finish a practice session or performance because you genuinely do not want to go home!

Imagine what it would be like to video your sessions as well and reflect on them to find the Moments of Perfection or MOPs (discussed soon) that are most aligned with the end-point pictures or clips that you have. Your confidence and self-belief would explode!

Having clarity about the final destination before you get underway with your coach is paramount. Never set sail without it and hope your skills will improve. You would still get better, but your progress would be slower than it could be, and more than likely quite painful and demoralising at times because you would feel like you were failing more than succeeding. Spend the time at the beginning building the clarity of the end point, and you will be repaid massively. Going 'over the top' about what the end point will look like is a good thing and something you won't regret.

LIVING IN THE REAL WORLD, NOT THE BULLSH*T WORLD

The most frequent finding with average to advanced athletes who come to see me for sports psychology input is that they have an overrated view of how good they are and how hard they are working! Most think their skill level is higher than it actually is, and most believe that they are living in the Green Box and working very hard. That is, most athletes at this level live in bullsh*t world. Few live in the real world regarding their current level of skill, competence and how hard they are working.

Golf is a great example of this, especially young golfers playing the 'bigger' events. Next time you go to such an event, ask for a player list that has the handicaps on it. Then, as the day progresses, look over the scoreboard when players start to come in. What I usually find is that some players do in fact play to their handicap, but not very many. Most play way outside their current rating. This can only mean one thing – they live in bullsh*t world and they lie! They either cheat by playing rounds with their mates and giving each other six footers for birdie or par, or they play all the easier courses and tournaments, which in turn gives them a false handicap rating that is lower than their actual ability.

I remember reading some interesting research during my early studies that looked at people's perceptions of their own attractiveness and general skill competency. What the research found was that the chronically depressed were the most accurate at rating their attractiveness and ability. It also found that most of the general population overrated their attractiveness and their general abilities or skills. That is, we think we are more attractive or handsome than we are and that we are more skilled than we are. Most of us are in fact pretty average – and ugly!

I am not trying to squash your confidence or self-image. I am actually helping you. Holding you to the real world and preventing you from going into the bullsh*t world is a vital part of reaching true self-belief and acceptance. This in turn is the key to unlocking your potential, gaining rapid skill development and having consistent and robust mental toughness under pressure.

The consequence of the bullsh*t mindset has huge ramifications on athletes when they train, practise and perform. During play, it means that most try things that they think they can pull off, but they seldom do as they just don't have the required skill set or physical strength. They may be successful in one out of fifty attempts, which they then falsely see as proof that they are competent at that skill. They don't (or won't) see that they have failed to make the attempt 49 times out of 50. This also helps explain why a lot of athletes, especially golfers, have terrible tempers, anger and rage when playing. Their external reality (e.g. in golf, taking double bogey or worse) does not match their overinflated internal view of themselves as a golfer. This is a common situation in golfers who come to see me. They are just unable to hold an 'objective' view of themselves, their skill and their competence, and when they play badly it becomes like an emotional wildfire.

Perhaps the most destructive impact of bullsh*t world, however, is that these athletes then think that they do not have to practise in a certain area because they are already good enough at it. I have seen this in all levels of athlete, from your regular weekend athletes (e.g. rugby and soccer players) to your seasoned professionals. Both levels have the tendency to avoid certain areas because they believe they have got them sorted, when non-emotional objective measurements and stats show that they have not!

Pathway 1 is living in the real world. Pathway 1 has no place or time for living in bullsh*t world – living there is the greatest enemy to uncovering potential. Pathway 1 demands robust self-accountability, because that is the key to ultimate self-acceptance. Self-acceptance sounds like this: 'I am as good as I am (low, medium or high ability) and I am not going to sugar-coat it; I will not judge it either' and 'It is just what it is'. In golf it might sound like this: 'I am a 25 handicap', 'I have a 10 per cent putting average from inside 10 feet', 'I hit 10 per cent of greens per round' and 'For me to get better I must live in the real world!' This type of mindset is seldom seen in athletes, however, or people in general for that matter, but when you do find an example of it, you have a person who is going to achieve great things. It is incredibly refreshing and inspiring to talk to a person like this, and to think like this yourself.

To hold yourself in the real world you must live objectively. Living objectively means that you never use the phrases: 'I think I am getting better' or 'I feel things are on track'. Athletes living in the real world know when they are on track and getting better because they use testing and keep stats. I cannot emphasise enough the importance of keeping stats and reviewing hard data.

Dean Eggers is a very successful New Zealand businessman with a deep love for golf. He currently manages some of New Zealand and Australia's top young professional golfers. When it comes to understanding what it takes to be world class in golf, he is one of the best. What I love about Dean is his absolute clarity in what he has to say. There is no embellishment, just the essentials! He had the following things to say when I asked him what he thought about planning and recording objective data.

PLANNING IS CRITICAL FOR SUCCESS

I believe to succeed in whatever you want to achieve in life, you actually have to plan to!

The key then is commitment to doing whatever is required to implement the plan.

Quality information showing that improvement is being achieved, and that you are getting closer to being the best in the world at all the little things that make up being that good (e.g. tee to fairway and fairway to green) is essential.

Dean Eggers

Dean Eggers takes some well-earned time out from caddying in Lucca, Italy.

The direct benefit you get from testing and reviewing stats is that it automatically requires you to live to your Pathway 1 philosophy and act from courage. Courage is required to overcome the fear of judgement and failing that often comes with testing and recording hard stats. Any emotion over your skill rating is removed and clear objective data is generated. This means you know exactly how good you are. Further, because you live by the Pathway 1 golden rule of 'no excuses' there is no hiding from the results, and you immediately start working on the right areas and doing the right things for the right period. Following stats also means that you do not spend too long in one area, as you know exactly the goal you are aiming for and when you have arrived at it, allowing you maximum productivity.

Gathering objective information means you have a clear baseline to start from and refer back to over time, and it gives you a true representation of your current reality or real world. Referring back to where you started on your journey provides an excellent opportunity to generate confidence in yourself and your plan as you reflect on and measure the shift. This also boosts belief in yourself that you can continue to grow, given how far you have already come.

Discussions around testing sessions and skill should be matter-of-fact and non-emotive. For example, when discussing improvement with your coach and other athletes, the discussion should revolve around current percentages and performance. Even though these discussions are non-emotive when they are about improvement they become incredibly powerful and drive up self-belief, which results in enthusiasm and motivation to practise more.

At times when stats and performance are getting worse, it is incredibly important to look at the figures in front of you without emotion. It is critical to look for and focus on overall trends. Resist getting caught up in one-off examples of when you performed badly (e.g. a missed tackle or a missed shot for goal when you were right in front and had the entire goal open). Often athletes get really focused on single examples of things going wrong, and then make sweeping changes to their plans as a result. When you are failing, remember Pathway 1 is the absence of excuses, give-up talk, reassurance seeking or looking for a 'magic bullet'. It is holding true to your philosophy (e.g. 'I would rather fail from a strong place than ever succeed from a weak one') and long-term plan, and then getting back to work. Having clear stats is critical to supporting you to succeed and fail strong. Their importance cannot be overstated!

The ability to be able to 'fail strong' and then quickly get back to work is possibly the most critical character trait needed in an athlete if they are to go on and challenge the best in the world. Ironically, one of our primary goals is to learn how to fail, so you can fully unleash from pure mind.

Testing Schedule

Testing should be locked into your weekly or monthly schedule and be the only time outside of performance where stats are really focused on during a standard practise week. Once testing periods are agreed upon with your coach, they are locked in. It's important to prevent yourself doing spontaneous, impulsive, doubt-driven or reassurance-seeking testing or video work in order to 'just make sure' things are on track.

The mind is a very sneaky thing and it will try to prove to you that you need to test and video more frequently than you actually do. Spontaneous, impulsive testing is the worst thing you can do. Your self-doubting mind will try to persuade you that testing and videoing frequently is the greatest thing to do. Ironically, when you test or video yourself 'just' to find out how you are going, and to reassure yourself that you are doing OK, it will only serve to increase the very doubt you sought to minimise, and consequently you will want to test and video again and again.

DEVELOPING THE STRATEGIC PLAN TO SUCCESS: EXERCISE 3

How Good Are You at Your Core Skills?

Sit down with your coach and ask them how you can test your current ability for each key core-skill area of the game.

If your dream is to be the best golfer in the world, then you will need to start using stats really effectively, as all your competition will be!

You need to record your shots during performances. You can use a golfing stat programme such as Shots to Hole to do this. TrackMan or the PuttLab system will help generate exact data on accuracy and technical proficiency of your golf swing and putting.

If you do not have access to these state-of-the-art systems and devices, you can establish a simple 10-ball testing exercise in a paddock or on the range. Make sure that the test can be accurately repeated. For example, you could put an upside-down umbrella at 65 metres and then draw rings around it at 1.5, 3 and 4.5 metres to act as circles like those you'd find on an archery target. You can then challenge yourself to see how many balls you can get into the umbrella. Record how far away your 10 balls land from the centre and work out your percentage.

Based on your discussions with your coach and others in your area, design your methods for generating data. Write them here:

Your results become the baseline against which to compare future tests.

BREAKING THE JOURNEY TO THE DREAM INTO NATURAL CYCLES

I often see athletes struggling with confidence issues. What usually surfaces during our sessions is that they have a deep sense that they are failing more than they are succeeding. This is due in part to how they define success, or what they see as most important, which we will discuss in more depth shortly. Feeling like they are failing is most often related to a tendency to compare current ability directly to the end point, which may be 15 years away (e.g. an 18-year-old five handicapper comparing himself against the current world number one in golf).

Low confidence also relates to a lack of patience and a deep desperation to achieve the end point now. The fact that they are not reaching their dream, and that they seem to be ageing incredibly quickly – 18 years old one day, 21 the next – they start to panic. This panic in turn leads to dread and self-doubt that they will never get there, and others somewhere out there will beat them to the 'prize'.

What is always lacking for these athletes is a strategic plan that spans backwards over time from their final destination to the here and now. My understanding of a strategic plan and its application is that it ensures that anything you do today is directly linked to the final destination.

BUILDING A STRATEGIC PLAN

A strategic plan breaks time down into blocks, with shorter and shorter blocks as you move from the final destination to the here and now. For example, if you have a 10-year plan to reach world number one, you could first look at the next five years and then break them down into one-year blocks. The year is a natural cycle, which makes it easy to plan for and to live to. Each year will have clear skill markers identifying just how good you should be by each time point. For example, you could set targets for how strong you will be in the gym, how fast you will be over 10 metres, what handicap you will be on, what events you will play by when, etc. It does not mean you absolutely have to achieve the actual targets set. They are merely markers that have been identified with your coach and support team to reflect what is expected to occur. Most importantly they will show you when your plan is working and you are on track.

I suggest that your plan has a lot of detail for the coming year, and general details for subsequent years. You should break your coming-year plan into quarters with a lot of detail in the first quarter, and then planning quarter by quarter throughout the year.

Each quarter can be broken down into months and weeks, then days and hours. You can have objectives or goals you want to achieve for a particular day, hour, half-hour or even minute.

TAKE CARE OF THE MINUTE AND THE HOURS (DAYS, WEEKS, MONTHS AND YEARS) WILL TAKE CARE OF THEMSELVES . . .

I prefer that players set achievable objectives (e.g. Monday morning – hit 50 x 60-degree full wedges using full routine and holding to 'deep practice') rather than outcome goals (e.g. hit all my 60-degree wedges within 15 feet this week) when establishing weekly and daily plans.

Lock in the key tournaments for the year, discussing any clashes with family or school commitments with your parents or coach. If at any point there is a clash, family and then school hold priority over sporting commitments. This is the approach I recommend to all families I work with, and it is the way that I will work with my own daughters when they get to a point where sport conflicts with family and school. Family and school must never be compromised by sport, in my view anyway. Sport must never become bigger than two things that are critical for long-term mental health: having great family relationships and doing well in school. Ironically, I have found that athletes who hold to family first, school second and sport third, and actually miss out on some key events in sport, end up better athletes than those who put sport at number one. It has a lot to do with keeping their feet anchored firmly to the ground about what is most important.

I suggest that you choose four key events for your strategic plan, one to represent the 'peak' for each quarter of the year. Each quarter should also be given specific outcome targets that you want to achieve (e.g. a top-three finish at the NZ Open; to win the

NZ Amateur Championship; to get selected for your provincial high-performance squad). These targets represent only one type of success; they are not the only measure of success, nor are they, in my view, the most important. The most important marker of success is *how* you go about training, practising and performing (e.g. whether you perform from courage and choose to LIVE your pursuit or whether you regress to performing from fear of bad outcomes as a careful coward). It is *how* you perform that determines the outcome and whether you achieve your potential consistently. I will discuss this in more depth shortly.

A strategic plan should also identify the key support people you will involve in your 'company', of which you are the CEO. Their roles, responsibilities and contributions (e.g. time or money) must be clearly documented and agreed to. If your parents are involved, they should not be required to contribute money. I strongly suggest you earn your own money, as when you earn it yourself, you feel pride for not bludging or being reliant on others. Your plan should also include dates for 'formal reviews'. A formal review is when you present stats and data to your support team or 'company' in order to review progress and, if required, refine or change the plan.

The Benefits of Building a Strategic Plan

The living strategic plan requires that you tick off daily objectives when completed and compare your work with the targets expected for that particular quarter. By doing so you will feel successful, which in turn will increase your confidence and self-belief, and give you a sense of achievement. This will then increase your ambition and enthusiasm to practise. The result is, in golf for example, increased quality ball strikes over time. That is the key to improvement and success, and achieving your dream.

The strategic plan and resulting structure will also support you to be patient. This patience will come from seeing, knowing and understanding the 'big picture'. This then allows you to stay calm and relaxed in the now and not feel like you have to achieve your dream today. You will enjoy the journey to the dream and immerse yourself fully in every little step along the way.

The power of the strategic plan is wonderfully highlighted in the following quote from one of New Zealand's top young female amateur golfers, Sarah Bradley. She explains how she is able to fully live each step along the way to her ultimate dream by getting crystal clear with her strategic plan.

THE POT OF GOLD BEHIND THE STRATEGIC PLAN

A friend once asked me if I could eat a whole elephant. I laughed and said, 'No way!' Her reply was, 'But what if you cut it up into small pieces?' I thought about it and said, 'Yes, but I would eat it slowly, bit by bit.' It challenged me to think about my vision – a vision so big that I was not clear where to start.

After hearing DG give a presentation on strategic planning and patience to our Waikato golf squad one evening, I had an 'ah-ha' moment!

It was about planning from the end point back, then starting with the very first step, committing to be the best in every area of my life, taking no shortcuts, and eating every little piece of this elephant-sized vision, one bite at a time. Going through the planning process resulted in me realising that my dream wasn't something that was huge and unattainable, but was a matter of me achieving the first very little step, then moving on to the next step and achieving that. By following that process, it would only be time before I reached the dream! All of a sudden the Impossible Dream became a very clear reality.

The most exciting part of this realisation was still to come, however! What I noticed was that the clearer I got about the strategic plan, the more and more patient I felt. Together the clarity and patience allowed me to feel a deep certainty that I would achieve my dream, and this resulted in me starting to feel like I had already done so. Most exciting was that it started to feel amazing every day, and with everything I did. I started to fully live my golf.

When put in this perspective, it's no longer about waiting for the day I achieve my dream. It's about this moment right now. It's about loving this wonderful opportunity I have ahead of me to fulfil my potential. It's about embracing the emotions of triumph and defeat, and building on them. Nothing makes me feel more alive.

When I realised this, I discovered I was already living out my dream (the pot of gold!) I will be patient, and bit-by-bit I will conquer this elephant-sized vision.

Sarah Bradley

THE IMPORTANCE OF THE WEEKLY SCHEDULE

The final part of this section looks specifically at the weekly schedule. In all of its simplicity, the weekly schedule is the most powerful 'psychological' tool I use. This is because behaviour does not lie! Many athletes and other people tell me that they are fully committed to their dream. I always reply, 'Great! Show me your weekly schedule.' The weekly schedule of a person who is paying the price and has a deep commitment to their dream is massively different from that of a person who is not. They are like night and day. People who are living in bullsh*t world, and are not committed to their dream, have a weekly schedule that is full of blanks and holes when they do nothing towards their dream – often nothing at all! They are saying the words, but their heart is not in it.

YOUR BEHAVIOUR, NOT YOUR WORDS, TELLS ME WHAT YOUR HEART REALLY WANTS!

Your weekly schedule would tell me if you were living Pathway 1 or Pathway 2. For example, if your weekly schedule showed lots of gaps or lots of 'wasted minutes' it would tell me one of two things: (1) that the dream you have verbalised is not actually your dream and you do not really want it (it could be that it is actually someone else's dream, like your parents') or (2) it is your dream, but self-doubt is robbing time through procrastination and avoidance. Either way, discussions revolving around the weekly schedule get this out on the table to allow open dialogue.

It is important that you establish a weekly routine that works for you. It should allow flexibility and provide clarity about what you will do, where you will do it, when you will do it and for how long. It should be so simple that a complete stranger should be able to pick it up and see what needs to be completed.

Below is a template that I use to plan my week. Every night I review the day that's just been and plan the next one. I have a thorough weekly schedule to show meetings and objectives for the week, then I go into deep detail on the day-by-day plan. My mentor has me record what I do with my day, hour-by-hour. I have to send him a copy every Monday by 5 p.m., otherwise I get a very short, sharp text or email from him asking why it is late. We also have a long-term strategic plan to guide my quarterly behaviours. Everything connects and we keep track to make sure all actions contribute to the yearly and longer-term five yearly goals, and the long-term vision. Everything I do counts!

Impossible Dream:

Pathway 1 Philosophy:

My Values: patience, planning, thoroughness, integrity, humility						Achieved
Daily Objectives:	1.					
	2.					
	3.					
		Mon	Tue	Wed	Thurs	Sun
5 a.m. through to 11 p.m.						
MOP Review						

Your weekly schedule should look like you are attacking the key areas in the right way and for the required time to achieve the desired outcome. An ideal weekly schedule should have a cover sheet with an outline of the entire week, as well as general objectives and goals. Then each day should have its own sheet, such as the form above, clearly outlining the day in detail. The weekly schedule should shout, 'I believe I will achieve my dream!'

DEVELOPING THE STRATEGIC PLAN TO SUCCESS: EXERCISE 4

Building Your Strategic Plan!

Block out at least one to two hours over the next week to sit down and write up your strategic plan to achieving your Impossible Dream.

Feel free to go online and download strategic plan templates from the Internet. There are many examples there for you to follow.

Arrange your first 'board meeting' with all the key people you want on your 'team' (e.g. parents, partner, coach, sports psychologist, nutritionist, trainer, etc).

Make sure you write the plan on your own before the meeting as this is living from Pathway 1. Getting someone else to do it is Pathway 2.

Present your strategic plan to your team in order to discuss it in depth and get feedback. Once you are all happy with the plan, assign roles and responsibilities, and then get to work.

Lock future review dates into your yearly planner. Nothing should get in the way of those meetings – they are that important. How often you meet will be determined by how big your dream is, who is on your support team, where they live and how often you are practising. The bigger the dream, the more often you should meet!

Doing this exercise from Pathway 1 means you accept that it will not be perfect, and that does not matter. What is important is that you write the plan and action your first board meeting. Spelling, grammar and format do not matter; what is in your heart and what is talked about are what matters. Get to work!

In summary, when you establish high clarity, you are on your way to success, whatever your dream may be. You unleash an unconscious energy that actually drags you towards the vision or dream. The end point must be clear enough so you can see it like a vivid video playing over in your mind, as well as taste it, feel it and touch it. You must have absolute clarity about how good you are right now with brutal Pathway 1 objectivity (i.e. data) and the steps needed to get to the dream.

You must be clear about each coming year's journey, and extra clear about the first quarter in the year, including specific steps with when, where, why and how, right down to each day. As you can see, there is an enormous amount of work that is required to establish this much detail. Most athletes will never reach their dream and, even sadder, never fully let go and fully live Pathway 1, because the underlying foundation is just too hard.

Subsequently, those with poor plans will end up meandering through their career, focused one day and slack the next, depending on their previous performance. If it was a good performance, they will be on top of the world, and if not, they will be struggling with transient depression. They will also remain 'reactive' across their career, spending time each day trying to fix problems from the last performance in order to get ready for the next one. They will never fully engage a proactive philosophy, building skill sets week by week in line with a long-term, well-thought-out plan. They will get to the end of their career and realise that they have failed from a weak place because they never really gave themselves a chance. They will know deep down that they never got focused enough.

Develop a thorough strategic plan to success and that will not happen to you! You will find your potential. You will either achieve your dream or you will not; either way, you will feel immense pride because you will know you did everything you could, and that is worth more than any amount of money can buy.

BUILDING POWERFUL NON-OUTCOME SUCCESS RULES

In addition to the fundamental biological need for water, food and oxygen, humans have a number of psychological needs that must be met for psychological health. Perhaps the most important of these needs is **the need to feel successful**. No matter who you are or how mentally tough you think you are, you must feel successful in order to have a healthy mind, confidence, self-esteem, enthusiasm and ambition. If you don't have a feeling of success, you feel either nothing at all, or you feel like you are failing. Both are as damaging as each other. To feel nothing is to wander through life never really experiencing joy or sadness, even during key life moments such as the birth of a child, the death of a parent or a daughter's wedding, and always remaining distant from others, never showing your true self. To feel as though you are constantly failing is the underlying cause of chronic self-doubt, fear of failing, performance anxiety (the dry retching just before you run out to play), unhappiness and, eventually, depression.

Feeling successful supports the growth of self-belief and, in turn, confidence. This leads to the development of ambition. Ambition ignites passion and enthusiasm to work hard, and the pursuit of excellence closely follows. These qualities are critical if a person is ever to be the best in the world or the best they can be, no matter what their dream. Given how important feeling successful is to reaching potential, it is critical you learn how to guarantee that you feel successful, no matter what the outcome, even when you are failing.

To feel successful even when failing! This is a massive statement to make. Most coaches laugh at me when I talk to them about this, and they often say, 'That is impossible; you don't know what you're talking about!' Not only do I disagree with them, but I then tell them that for their athletes to truly unleash their minds they need to take the potential of failing out of their reality, and learn not to care about it. They will still 'fail', and often, but whether they focus on the failing or on *how* they did what they did (non-outcome focus) will ultimately determine how they feel about the final outcome (usually pride if feeling successful or shame and embarrassment if feeling a 'failure'). Our experiences in the world are absolutely determined by how we think about them. Whether you are 'successful' or a 'failure' is entirely up to how you think and what you focus on. The only time you should feel unsuccessful and like you had failed, in this powerful 'non-outcome' mindset, would be if your effort or attitude were poor, or you gave up.

The most exciting thing of all about living with non-outcome success rules is that the actual outcome is entirely within your control. Something very special happens when an athlete deeply connects to a belief that success equals non-outcome expectations e.g. 'to give it my all' or 'to go for it'. It is in this mindset that athletes are able to quickly drop into instinctive performance mode, in which their mind enters a pure state or emotional zone.

It is impossible to drop in there when connected to outcome thinking. It is in this zone that athletes reach their potential and achieve optimal performance and performance consistency.

This next section steps you through how to achieve a mindset that is deeply connected to non-outcome success rules. In many ways, it is the most important part of this book. It is impossible to fully unleash your mind and obtain pure Pathway 1 courage if you are in a success-equals-outcome mindset. Hence, everything we do in this book hinges on this critical outlook: defining success, or what is most important, in terms of how you do what you do.

Here is a brief passage from Lisa Carrington on the importance of holding strongly to a non-outcome performance mindset to achieve your deepest potential.

THE SPIRITUAL POWER OF BEING FREE OF PERFORMANCE OR OUTCOME EXPECTATIONS

When I drop into this special place [her performance zone], whether I am racing or even training, it is where I am completely free of expectation, results and outcome. It is kind of a neutral place where my actions are a true expression of who I am without fear of judgement or result, which inevitably is an outcome. This special place is somewhere I go when I need to achieve important things, when it is a situation that scares me, like the Olympics or world champs. I believe when a person is free from outcome and expectation they will truly be the best version of themselves.

Lisa Carrington

Even on a standard training day, it is critical to remain linked to non-outcome success rules to get the best out of a session. It is fine to have 'targets' for the day or the period you are working on, but they are just that – targets – and although a form of success, they should never become the 'most important' measure of success.

When you look at the most successful people in sport and life, they seem to have mastered this mindset. They take positives from negative circumstances, they see failing as their best friend and embrace it with open arms, and they seem to be constantly smiling. For example, in golf, people with this mindset look like they are from another universe! They make eight on a par three, but when you ask them about it, they say, 'Didn't you see that last putt? That eight could have been a ten real easy! I was so proud with my courage to hold to my pre-shot routine with that putt, especially under that much pressure.' What is most inspiring is that these people actually mean what they are saying and deeply believe it. It is not a front to cover deeper anguish or disappointment in the result.

These people actually removed 'failing' from their vocabulary, and because they do not focus on it, they actually extinguish it from their reality. As a result, they live life to the full. 'I will express myself' is their core Pathway 1 philosophy. They make 'expressing themselves' the <u>most important</u> thing in the world. They do not fear failing because in their minds they have made it the least important thing. It still exists, but it is so irrelevant, it essentially does not exist for them because it gets no time in their minds. This is where the real magic begins to happen – when outcome is put way down the <u>most-important</u> list, and how you do what you do, e.g. express yourself, is considered the most critical thing above anything else. It is in this place that your mind truly starts to unleash!

I keep underlining 'most important' because I want you to make a critical connection. When we start discussing 'success rules' what we are talking about is what you consider to be most important to you. You can place outcome as most important, and everything you say and do will look massively different from someone who places non-outcome expectations as most important. I always use the term 'most important' when discussing success rules with athletes, families or coaches, and non-sporting clients to help them understand what I am actually talking about. Success rules will be explained in more detail shortly.

NON-OUTCOME THINKING – THE HARDEST ROAD TO LIVE ON!

People often say to me when talking about non-outcome success rules and not focusing on failing, that I am encouraging athletes to take the easy road and be soft on themselves because they never look at where they fail.

Ironically, athletes who live fully in this world where they place outcome as the least important thing always seem to place effort as the most important (i.e. success equals effort). They also usually place planning, hard work, feedback and learning high up on the list of importance. This combination of elements is what the great long-term repeat world champions are made of. Their pride in how they apply themselves is far more important than the outcome itself!

In essence they become values driven, not urge driven. Value-driven athletes always outdo urge-driven athletes. They live on the hard road and love it.

Further, a non-outcome mindset prevents people dropping into bullsh*t world, thinking that they did well after a victory when they did not give 100 per cent effort. If you have outcome as your key marker of success, you could feel quite pleased with a result (e.g. winning a rugby championship) when actually it was not a good performance because your effort or attitude was poor. Holding to the mindset I am discussing in this chapter removes that risk. It forces you to be accountable for your performance and all your actions.

The effort and sense of accountability needed to fully live by this pathway is massive. For most, it is just too hard, and is why they never fully embrace Pathway 1 or unleash their mind.

EXPLAINING SUCCESS RULES

Whether somebody feels successful or not depends on how their behaviour or experiences compare to their own standards, demands or expectations. If, for example, they meet their own standards with the score they get on a round of golf or in a test, then they feel successful. If the score does not measure up, they often feel that they have failed and then they feel like a failure. I call these standards, demands or expectations success rules, because they reflect rules that must be met for a person to feel successful and happy. They are what that person considers <u>most important</u>. Success rules can be helpful or unhelpful.

Helpful Success Rules

Helpful success rules are incredibly robust and set you up to feel successful. As mentioned earlier, the best success rules even make it possible to feel successful when failing, and as a result make it impossible for you to feel like a failure. You may still fail, and will likely still experience feelings such as frustration or disappointment, and even grief or anger, albeit fleeting. This is normal when you are engaged in something dear to your heart. Your perception of the event is such, however, that you do not feel like a failure, and may even feel successful when you have failed, because your effort was world class!

Consequently, helpful success rules result in a robust growth in confidence and self-belief across time, even when failing or going through adversity. A direct by-product of feeling successful is a greater motivation to do more practice, thereby actually increasing opportunities to perform well and win by being more and more prepared. Subsequently, you feel more and more successful over time. This facilitates a beautiful, progressive cycle of action and learning that drives up skill and performance, and then confidence and self-belief. Hence these types of success rules are very helpful!

> **'SUCCESS IS PEACE OF MIND THAT IS THE DIRECT RESULT OF SELF-SATISFACTION IN KNOWING YOU DID YOUR BEST TO BECOME THE BEST THAT YOU ARE CAPABLE OF BECOMING.'**
> **JOHN WOODEN**

John Wooden is widely considered to be the greatest coach of all time. His records are incredible: 10 US National University basketball titles in 12 years, seven in a row, four years unbeaten! Given the size of the university basketball competition, it is considered harder to win this Championship than to win the NBA. Perhaps the most powerful element when looking at what made John Wooden tick is how he defined success. Not once in his career was he heard using the word 'winning'. He did not let it enter his vocabulary or his mind. He saw winning as a result or outcome of 'what someone did', and something that was not in their control. He felt that you could play your best and lose, or play your worst and win, so why would you waste your time focusing on the outcome when it could potentially give you a false picture of events anyway? He also thought that 'outcome-thinking', such as focusing on the score, actually got in the way of performing to your potential and doing your job. Winning to John Wooden was of secondary importance. Sounds crazy, but there is a powerful lesson in here for all of us, especially those who play or perform at the highest levels. Make no mistake, however – John still loved competing and winning, but it was simply not as important as doing one's best.

A POWERFUL LESSON ON SUCCESS FROM THE MASTER

The most powerful lesson I have learnt about the true nature of success came when I was reading the transcript from one of John Wooden's interviews later in his coaching career.

This particular interview highlighted how Wooden struggled with the common view of success as winning. He became quietly annoyed with the interviewer, who was asking him about winning and why he was never heard to talk about it. Now, John Wooden's 'annoyed' was mild compared to most people's, as he was such a peaceful and respectful man, but I inferred his feelings from the frank tone of his reply.

The following is my paraphrase of what he said:

'Look, let's get this out of the way before we go any further. I am deeply competitive and love winning; in fact, you will probably struggle to find a more competitive person, but that is not why I played or coached. I played and coached because I love the game! I love giving my best at whatever I do because that is true success; I let the outcome and results take care of themselves and they do not even enter my mind. I chose to focus instead on what I can control, and that is all the little things that I do and say.'

John Wooden's definition of success aligns with my own thoughts and reinforces for me why I spend so much time and effort working with people to establish powerful non-outcome success rules.

Wooden's success rule is very helpful as it allows a person to feel successful even when failing, making mistakes or losing, as long as they give it their best. Note how giving or doing your best (i.e. 100 per cent effort) is totally in your control. That is the secret to a 'perfect' success rule; it is fully in your control, and consequently you determine if you are successful or not.

HOW YOU KNOW YOU HAVE A GREAT SUCCESS RULE

A great success rule will make you feel like you want to go and train, practise or perform right now! It will give you an uplifted sense of spirit and belief that you can achieve your potential. The true test of whether you have the right success rule comes when you fail, not succeed. A great success rule will support you to move through failing quickly, with little, if any, distress and without dropping into depression, despair, regret or anger. It will lead you to have a consistent emotional base over time, rather than the highs and lows that come with focusing on outcome. It will be this peace of mind after succeeding or failing that will have you back to work at 8 a.m. on Monday morning rearing to go.

A great success rule will lead you to reminisce on moments when your character was strong, even if these include performances during which everything went wrong. It will also allow you to focus on good outcomes inside losing performances (e.g. in golf, a last putt for double bogey that if you had not made would have resulted in you shooting 100). A poor success rule will lead you to ruminate on all the lost opportunities.

The speed with which you move through failing and adversity will tell you whether you define success based on outcome or effort. If it is on outcome, it is likely that you will find failing and adversity a struggle, experiencing powerful negative emotions such as anger, frustration and desperation that will feel like they control you and take a long time to get over. Consequently, you will lose valuable time and focus when starting practice again, as both will be compromised.

Unhelpful Success Rules

Unhelpful success rules are the complete opposite of helpful ones. They result in feelings of failure and, as a result, frequently lead to an increase in self-doubt, fear of failure and performance anxiety. The worst success rules lead you to feel like a failure even when you are winning or performing incredibly well – crazy as that sounds! A common finding among some of the most talented young athletes in New Zealand is that they feel as if they are failing even though they are some of the best in the country, and often the world. This is just astonishing, and incredibly sad.

This is how unreachable success rules work in your mind: you do something; your mind reviews what you just did and compares it with your expectations of what needs to happen for that act to be considered a success; if your results do not match the underlying rule or expectation your mind fires back, 'YOU FAILED!'

Imagine what it is like to be told repeatedly, 'YOU FAILED! No, that is not good enough! YOU FAILED! YOU FAILED!' That is exactly what happens in your mind when you have unhelpful success rules. In most areas of high performance, people fail thousands of times a week. Imagine the powerful negative impact that has on someone's mind. No one can retain confidence or self-belief when confronted with that sort of constant feedback; it erodes self-worth and self-esteem.

Repeated failing and feeling like a failure quickly leads to feeling down or melancholy. Further, it is not uncommon for this to lead to depression. Melancholy and depression in an athlete decreases their desire to practise, which results in less time spent doing the most important thing. This consequently increases the chances of them performing badly, resulting in them feeling even more like a failure. The athlete falls into a vicious 'failure cycle' that is incredibly hard to break. Hence these sorts of success rules are unhelpful. They probably should be called 'hand grenades' as they will blow up a dream very quickly!

The following is a story that shows just how powerful unhelpful success rules are at negatively influencing behaviour. It is my own experience of parenting my eldest daughter when she was approximately two years old.

One weekday afternoon, I was busy cleaning the dishes as my

wife was expected home from work in the next half an hour or so. The lawns were long and my father was coming to visit that weekend. There was not enough time to get everything done and the weather was turning for the worse. I was under pressure, and feeling it. I was stressed. This pressure and stress was coming from the threat that I would not meet my success rules – the things that needed to occur for me to feel like an 'adequate and competent husband and son'.

The following list summarises the deep success rules I had back then, or what I thought was most important:
1. I have to be perfect (i.e. WIN and not LOSE) in everything I do, especially to please my wife and father.
2. I must not be imperfect, I must not make any mistakes and I must not have one thing go wrong (as my wife and father would then judge me as less worthy or manly, and a useless fake).
3. I must avoid others seeing me as not measuring up because they will think I am a useless fake and not as good as I think I am.

When looking at the success rules or demands I had on myself, it is instantly obvious they are unhelpful. They set me up to feel like a failure, and often; simply because it was impossible to meet the standards they set. Even worse was that these success rules left me feeling like a failure even when I was achieving great things in my life, as I was never perfect or good enough, and I felt that I could always be better. The stressed emotions I was feeling in the story above were a direct result of the threat that I would fail (again) to achieve my impossible standards, expectations or success rules.

Let us continue with the story. My two-year-old daughter was tired and grizzly. She started to cry and wandered into the kitchen as I was trying to finish the dishes. Not only did this situation place me at risk of not achieving the demands I had put on myself as a parent, a husband and a man, it also directly threatened the success rules or demands I had in place for my children and how they needed to behave 'for me'.

Here are the success rules I had in place for my daughter at that time:
1. Children must behave like adults; my daughter must therefore behave like me.
2. Children must not cry or grizzle.
3. Children must never misbehave.
4. Children must listen the first time.
5. Children must show instantaneous obedience.
6. Children must behave perfectly all of the time.

You can probably predict what sort of behaviour I was about to show based on the success rules I had set for myself and my child. I was like a bomb ready to go off!

Instead of stopping doing the dishes and giving her a cuddle, I was grumpy and short. I said to her that she needed to stop crying or she could go to her room. She increased her crying, turned around, toddled to the door in between the kitchen and the foyer and head-butted the glass plane, smashing it. I stopped washing the dishes!

This single event was, and remains, one of the most critical in all my life. It led me to reflect deeply on what had happened, and it was this self-reflection that resulted in me really targeting success rules in everything I did from that point on.

This story highlights how success rules do more than govern how we feel before, during and after an event. They directly control what we do in any circumstance; they govern our behaviour completely. Most people operate 'unconsciously' from moment to moment. When operating unconsciously, behaviour is completely controlled by underlying success rules.

The demands I had on my daughter and myself were like dynamite waiting to go off. Looking back, I can now see why I always felt unhappy as a dad, a husband and a man. I always felt under pressure, day in and day out, and as if something bad were about to happen. Even when things were going well, I felt constant

Here is my daughter aged 10 years. What she taught me when she was two years old ended up being the most important lesson of my entire life! It was because of this one moment that I made personal changes that have resulted in the life I lead today. It saved my marriage and my family. It was that massive.

worry that just around the corner the wheels would fall off, and something would go seriously wrong. I had felt this way for as long as I could remember, especially when I'd played representative golf as a teenager. I'd felt unsuccessful and as if I were a failure, even though I was achieving great things and was a very good athlete across a number of sports.

I can now also see how these success rules, when applied to my wife, almost cost me my marriage. It was because my standards were so high and so linked to 'outcome' that I felt as though: (a) I was constantly failing or on the edge of failing, and as a result struggled with a deep sense of shame and being a failure; and (b) my children and wife were never meeting the success rules I had for them, and therefore were always failing me, leaving me constantly grumpy and angry with them.

BUILDING POWERFUL NON-OUTCOME SUCCESS RULES: EXERCISE 1

Uncover Your Current Success Rules in Life!

Before we look at your sport and performance, let's look at your life and what sort of success rules you may be living by.
Ask yourself:

What needs to happen in my life for me to feel happy _____?

For example, if you go to school, then write 'at school' at the end of the question; if you are married then write 'in my marriage' or 'with my wife or husband'; and if you work write 'at work'. Then brainstorm some answers.

Example Answers
At school: get A grades for ALL my papers; to have cool friends; to be the most liked at school; to get dux and/or be sportsperson of the year.

With my wife: she listens first time; she does what I want her to do; she never questions me or tells me what to do; she is perfect; she looks stunning; she loves me absolutely and proves that I am her number one.

At work: my boss always thanks me; I am allowed to do what I want; I get a pay rise every year; I get promoted before anyone else does; people do what I suggest at planning meetings; I have my name mentioned in the work newsletter.

When you have brainstormed your answers, look over them and see if there are any unhelpful themes similar to my old ones, setting you up to feel like a failure (e.g. demanding that you and those around you are perfect).

Make any general comments to yourself based on your own self-reflection (i.e. what you may have uncovered about yourself).
For example: no wonder I feel this way so often because I am demanding everyone around me to do it my way. No wonder my children seem nervous around me when I am unhappy and people hold me at arm's length and do not trust me or tell me the truth – they are afraid of me.

How My Real-Life Example Applies to Sport

I am constantly amazed at how closely my own story fits the stories of many of the elite athletes I now work with. Many of them are incredibly successful, yet come to me with depression, self-doubt and performance anxiety, and deep down feel like a fake and/or an utter failure. They feel like this because their lives are being polluted by the same sorts of success rules that almost destroyed my marriage, family and life.

We often see athletes throwing tantrums! How often do we see golfers and tennis players sulk after bad shots, for example? These behaviours are all too common on the sporting courts, fields and courses around the world. Most athletes, when talking about these issues, feel powerless and unable to control them. It is as though they become a different person and a 'red mist' descends over them. These behaviours are a direct product of unhelpful success rules that set them up to feel like a failure rather than a success. These athletes would all have outcome-based success rules that are so extreme and unrealistic (e.g. success equals winning every time; perfection with every shot; absolute control over every shot; make no mistakes) that they feel like a failure every time they perform. It suffocates potential because even when playing well and/or winning, they never feel good enough. The demands and expectations that they set become like a heavy weight on their shoulders that eventually will wear them down and drive them to hate the sport they used to love.

Here is a great example from the current world number five in squash, New Zealand's Joelle King, which has strong connections to my story above.

THE WEIGHT OF THE WORLD ON MY SHOULDERS ONE DAY TO FREE SPIRIT THE NEXT!

When I walked into David's house eight months ago, I had the weight of the world on my shoulders when I played. 'I have to win', 'I can't lose' were often the thoughts running through my mind before, during and after my matches. I could feel my own mindset suffocating my potential! It was like a hand brake, and I had no control over it. It was holding me back in matches that I knew I should be winning, and had me playing well under my best, especially when it counted!

There was one particular match during which this occurred, and that was haunting me. 'I was up 6–0 in the fifth to the world number one and choked,' were my exact words. 'I could have been number four or three,' were my exact thoughts. I couldn't even watch the replay of the match without cringing and squirming.

'How did I lose that match?' I kept asking myself for weeks and

even months afterwards. I just could not shake it from my mind!

It wasn't until I met David and told him about this, to which he replied, 'I DON'T CARE WHAT THE SCORE WAS,' that my mind started to look at things in a very different way.

I guess you could say I was a bit taken aback by his response, but after sitting at his house for an hour and a half listening to him, I just wanted to learn more. Together we set in place plans and goals that I was going to live by and ensure whilst training and living. A key focus was for me to master dropping into a space where I did not care about the outcome, but cared deeply about accessing a pure instinctual feeling and just going for it.

The shift was amazing! It is still a work in progress, but I am finding new levels and I have a hunger to play and train the best I can. I now look at a match that before would have had me feeling scared and sick with nerves as a new challenge.

Playing with no stress or tightness: well, this was something new. Even losing to the world number three was exciting. It sounds strange, but that loss helped me to learn things and improve, and a new challenge was set. I felt like I could never fail!

In November 2013, I walked back into David's house and told him about a recent match:

'I was 8-2 down in the first and it happened: I dropped into this place I had been hunting where I did not care about the outcome. It was the most amazing feeling. My body was loose and I knew exactly what to do next; it was pure. I didn't really know what the score was until I shook her hand. For three sets I had the feeling. Did I win or lose? The crazy thing is now, 'I DON'T CARE WHAT THE SCORE WAS!'

Now my recaps from tournaments and judgements of myself are no longer based on whether I won or lost. It's something so much more that is leading and pushing me to find that 'feeling' every time I do anything, especially when I step on court, whether that is to train or play. Of course I still want to win – deeply! That is a given. But I want that feeling more. It fires my soul and feeds my spirit!

Joelle King

Joelle's story shows two things. Firstly, it highlights how suffocating a 'success-equals-winning' mindset can be, shutting down potential, especially at the key moments in sport when an athlete should be expressing themselves and often finishing the opposition off! Secondly, it vividly shows the dramatic shift that can occur in an athlete's mind and performance when they disconnect from outcome and stop 'caring about it', instead seeking simply to express themselves from pure courage (i.e. making how they do what they do most important).

Now that you have heard how changing your success rules can unleash your mind and potential in sport at the highest level on the world stage, let's discuss how you can uncover the success rules you currently have in place for your sport or other pursuit (e.g. music). If you are reading this book to help with your general life or business rather than sport or other pursuits, you may want to move on to the next section: 'How to Change Unhelpful Success Rules.' However, you might still find the next section interesting, so feel free to read on if you wish.

HOW DO YOU UNCOVER YOUR SPORT/ PERFORMANCE SUCCESS RULES?

Below are some unhelpful success rules held by many of the golfers I have worked with over the years. Although this is a golfing example, the answers can be applied quite readily to other areas (e.g. music and other sport codes).

These rules were uncovered by asking the golfers, 'What needs to happen in golf for you to feel happy when you perform?' and then following up their answers with, 'And what else?' when they seemed to have run out of ideas.

Examples of Unhelpful Success Rules in Golf:
1. Sixty-five. I have to shoot 65 to feel happy or successful after a round of golf. (Note: 65 is a world-class score, and getting close to a perfect round.)
2. I have to have complete control over the ball flight for every shot.
3. I have to make no three-putts.
4. I have to hit all my fairways.
5. I have to make no mistakes.
6. I have to learn my lessons from mistakes immediately on the course and not make them again. What I am saying is that it is OK for me to make a mistake once, but not twice. To make the same mistake twice is absolutely unacceptable and stupid!

The negative power of these success rules should hit home when reading them. It is easy to see how these rules demand that the golfers are perfect! It is also easy to see that such negatively powerful success rules will result in the golfers feeling as if they are failing more than they are succeeding. For example, with the first player, who had been referred to me with depression, his success rule meant that when he shot 66 or 67, he felt as though he had failed because he always thought his round could have been better.

It is also easy to make a direct link between these rules and the ones that almost destroyed my family and life so many years ago. These young golfers felt as though they were failing more than they were succeeding, even though they were playing professionally or were some of the best amateur golfers in New Zealand. How crazy that our top young talent felt more like losers than winners, more like failures than successes. This is a result of one thing: underlying unhelpful success rules.

Further, if they had held on to these success rules, those players would never have been able to enter true Pathway 1. Their mindset would always have been Pathway 2, with deep self-doubt and fear of playing badly and failing, especially under great pressure. This would have been due to their minds working hard to try not to break their success rules. The Pathway 2 mindset is driven by an avoidance of mucking up or losing rather than letting go and playing to win. It is critical that unhelpful success rules like those listed here are changed before an athlete can unleash their mind and 'let go', with pure Pathway 1 courage.

BUILDING POWERFUL NON-OUTCOME SUCCESS RULES: EXERCISE 2

Uncovering Your Current Success Rules in Sport/Other Pursuits

Now it is time for you to uncover your success rules in your area of pursuit.

Ask yourself:

> **What needs to happen in _____ (e.g. music, cricket, athletics – whatever your pursuit is) for me to feel happy when I perform?**

List all your answers here. When your mind goes blank, simply ask yourself, 'What else needs to happen for me to feel happy?' Keep going until you have listed everything that comes up in your mind.

Now, read back over this list. What have you learnt about yourself? Write a few comments to yourself here (e.g. no wonder I always feel as though I am failing, I am demanding that I be perfect):

A REAL-LIFE EXAMPLE OF HOW DESTRUCTIVE OUTCOME SUCCESS RULES ARE IN SPORT

I recently caught up with a golfer I worked with several years ago, when she was 18. The following were her success rules at that time:

Success rule 1: Sixty-five. I have to shoot 65 to feel happy or successful after a round of golf.

Success rule 2: I have to have complete control over the ball flight for every shot.

This player was unable to consistently relax and express herself when she played. She was overly technical and tried her hardest to be perfect with every shot. She was very talented but inconsistent, and she struggled to turn opportunity into victory. She would often freeze up when in front, then blow leads and end up losing by one or two shots.

 She hardly ever felt truly successful and, if she did, it lasted only a short time before she tumbled back into a deep sense of dread that she was going to fail the next time she went out. She felt constantly frustrated and angry. She felt as though she was never good enough. Not surprisingly, she often experienced low moods and depression, despite publicly appearing positive and happy. She was churning up inside, and the game was slowly destroying her!

 She agreed that she was deeply linked to outcome, but disagreed that this need to perform actually prevented her from reaching her potential. She was convinced that it actually motivated her. What I failed to do was to find a way to support her to see that this was not the case. Our working relationship ended at that point. Back then she held strongly to the belief that she needed to focus on score to drive her practice and enthusiasm to play, and to motivate herself to be competitive at events.

 Over the last two to three years, I have kept a quiet eye on her progress from afar. It has not gone well. She has continued to under perform. I recently bumped into her at a tournament and we ended up chatting about her progress. During this discussion, she asked me what I had been working on. Over the subsequent 30-minute chat, I talked about how disconnecting from outcome and building powerful process success rules based on effort, not score, was becoming the cornerstone of my work. Her reply to me was this: 'How can you motivate yourself if you do not focus on score?'

Her question shows just how locked in to outcome she continued to be and how, even after struggling so much over the past few years, she continued to apply the same recipe to her golf. Her answer also illuminated why she actually plays golf: because of a 'need' to be perfect. She continues to pursue 65 and perfect ball control in every round, and with every practice session. There is nothing in her success rules about playing for the love of the game or just to play, nor is there anything about being motivated by learning and challenging herself (e.g. by living on the edge of bogey) to see just how good she can become.

Terrible as it is to say, this golfer is not going to make it, not with her current mindset. Unless she adjusts her success rules she is doomed because she will spend all her energy trying to squeeze out the last five per cent of improvement that will require eighty-five per cent of her time to achieve – time she just does not have!

More destructive, however, psychologically her unconscious mind will be motivated by trying to avoid being imperfect. Now, when the unconscious mind tries to avoid mucking it up, it automatically locks itself into what I call a 'Moment of Sh*t' (MOS) mindset – focusing on learning from past errors. The journey becomes frustrating, painful and depressing. She will continue to feel as though she is failing more than succeeding, and this will result in her hating the very game she should be loving.

HOW DO YOU CHANGE UNHELPFUL SUCCESS RULES?

Returning to my parenting story: it was my reflection on my parenting of my eldest daughter that really catapulted me into working more deeply with success rules. This one experience initiated years of working on how best to support athletes to build powerful unleashing success rules. Over time, I realised that we can choose any success rule we desire. For example, had I had any of the following success rules or demands in the same situation with my daughter, my behaviour and the outcome would have been totally different:

1. Children should always express themselves.
2. Children are supposed to cry.
3. Children are supposed to grizzle.
4. Children should be put before lawns or dishes.
5. Children must be loved when tired and distressed, not punished.
6. Fathers should spend more time playing with their children each day than cleaning or mowing lawns.
7. Children should have fun every day.
8. The house should be untidy at the end of the day.
9. Dishes should only be done when the children are in bed.

SUCCESS EQUALS HAVING FUN AND LAUGHING!

This is the success rule I forced myself to start living by from that moment with my daughter going forward. This is what I made the most important thing in the fathering of my children and my relationship with my wife. It saved my relationship with my daughter and resulted in me relaxing as a dad, a husband and a person. It saved my life, it was that massive!

I then committed to being successful every day by finding a way to make my daughter laugh and have fun. I simply asked

The two girls at home in Hamilton. My eldest daughter and I have a pretty special relationship now, and all because I started walking around the house farting when I got out of bed in the mornings! Crazy how something so small can be so powerful. That is how important success rules are.

myself what having fun parenting my daughter would look like and how I could make her laugh. I brainstormed the answers. Here are some examples I came up with:

1. Getting up in the morning and walking around the house farting really loudly. As you know, little children laugh incredibly hard when anything like this happens.
2. Chasing and tickling her.
3. Having ice cream for breakfast at the weekends.
4. Setting up the tent in the lounge and going 'home camping' once a week.
5. Going to the park on a Saturday for the whole morning and letting her play for as long as she wanted.
6. Letting her be the 'boss' for half a day, during which time I had to do everything she said. (No money allowed on this day, however. It usually involved dressing and undressing dolls!)

The ability to change behaviour by choosing the right success rules applies as much to sport as it does to parenting and life in general. Athletes can choose the success rules or expectations and demands they place on themselves. That in turn means that they can choose success rules that guarantee they will feel successful, no matter how badly they perform.

If an athlete can establish demands and standards that force them to focus on *how* they do what they do, and not what the outcome is, they will generate powerful success rules. For example, imagine what sort of athlete you would be if you performed from the following success rules.

Success equals:
1. playing from my Pathway 1 philosophy
2. sticking to my performance plan
3. putting the ball firmly along the line (in golf)
4. being courageous when scared or doubtful
5. emptying the 'mind tank'
6. playing on the edge of hitting the ball out of court (in tennis)
7. taking risks
8. working hard
9. failing (one of Michael Jordan's)
10. having fun (my parenting one).

Compare this type of athlete with the golfer I described earlier in this section (i.e. success equals shooting 65; make no three-putts; hit all my fairways).

The ten success rules above support an athlete to be mentally tough, especially under pressure, as they are focused on what they can control and get themselves to do, rather than the outcome of the situation. They experience much more fun, even when performing under the greatest pressure. This does not mean that they don't care about winning and performing well, of course they should still want this to occur, but it is far down on the list of importance for them.

For athletes at the highest level wanting to win is a given. There is no need to write it down let alone mention it. It is wired in! These athletes also know that for them to execute well, they must be relaxed, calm and confident, which occurs more easily if they disconnect from outcome. They no longer *need* to win or perform well to feel good about themselves, and that has many positive benefits for performing from a free and pure mindset.

'I HAVE NEVER BEEN AFRAID OF FAILING, BECAUSE I KNEW THAT FOR ME TO BE TRULY SUCCESSFUL WHEN IT COUNTED, I FIRST HAD TO LEARN HOW TO FAIL! THE MORE I FAILED AND EMBRACED FAILING, THE GREATER I BECAME AT JUST LETTING GO . . . FAILING BECAME SUCCESS BECAUSE I KNEW THAT ULTIMATE SUCCESS WAS JUST AROUND THE CORNER!'

PARAPHRASED FROM SEVERAL MICHAEL JORDAN INTERVIEWS ON YOUTUBE

BUILDING POWERFUL NON-OUTCOME SUCCESS RULES: EXERCISE 3

Establishing Powerful Helpful Success Rules in Sport/Other Pursuits

To establish powerful helpful success rules for your pursuit, ask the following question:

What standards or expectations could I set myself that would guarantee that I felt successful no matter what my score was or how well or poorly I performed?

Some examples are:
1. Keep injecting the LION (Pathway 1 philosophy), no matter what.
2. Stick to my game plan.
3. Work really hard at going deeply into my pre-shot routine (golf/tennis).
4. Empty the tank and give it my all.
5. Be patient.
6. Relax.
7. Have fun and laugh.
8. Go for it.
9. Learn something that will help fine tune my training.

Brainstorm a list here:

Now go through each one, testing how robust it is. You can test the robustness of a success rule by asking yourself, 'How would I feel using this success rule on my worst day?' If the answer is, 'Successful,' then you have a great success rule.

It is OK to have multiple helpful success rules.

List your preferred one(s) here:

1. _____

2. _____

3. _____

To help inject them into your game/pursuit ask yourself the following question:

What would my new success rule(s) look like in _____?

For example, if you play tennis and your new success rule is 'Have fun' ask yourself what having fun would look like when you were playing tennis. You could then go through every part of the training or tournament day and identify what would make it fun. For example:
1. Wearing a very bright, funny coloured shirt and hat.
2. Playing fun, competitive games with my coach to help warm up.
3. Having music playing.
4. Smiling at mum after every good shot.
5. Setting up the tent and area where we sit during the day in a really comfortable way and taking a trailer and couch along.

The list can be endless and only limited by your imagination. The key is that all your answers must strongly link to what you have defined as success.

POWERFUL NON-OUTCOME SUCCESS RULES THAT GUARANTEE ATHLETES FEEL SUCCESSFUL

Here are some actual success rules that athletes I have worked with now live and play by. As you read over them, imagine what these athletes would be feeling as they prepare to execute.

1. Choose to live and express myself under pressure (therefore the greater the pressure the more exciting).
2. Be relaxed/calm under pressure.
3. Hit the ball with deep intent of where I intend it to go (golf/tennis).
4. Follow my plan.
5. Embrace and sprint towards pressure – going for it.
6. Learn something.
7. Play shot from courage and my Pathway 1 philosophy (tennis).
8. Fail/succeed strong.
9. Never give up.
10. Putt strongly along my line (golf).
11. Don't care about outcome at all and live by the F-IT philosophy.
12. Have fun and laugh!

Imagine demanding these expectations from yourself during training, practice and performance, and compare them to the list of the player I discussed earlier in this section, i.e.:

1. Sixty-five. I have to shoot 65 to feel happy or successful after a round of golf. (Note: 65 is a world-class score, and getting close to a perfect round.)
2. I have to have complete control over the ball flight for every shot.
3. I have to make no three-putts.
4. I have to hit all my fairways.
5. I have to make no mistakes.
6. I have to learn my lessons from mistakes immediately on the course and not make them again. What I am saying is that it is OK for me to make a mistake once, but not twice. To make the same mistake twice is absolutely unacceptable and stupid!

I know which mindset I would bet on for who would win gold, the Masters or a local club championship! What most stands out in the first list above is the absence of outcome and that all the expectations are totally in the players' control. The athletes can make each of these happen, and in turn make themselves feel and be successful! That is the secret and beauty of great success rules.

Athletes living from this mindset would be experiencing deep calm, certainty and clarity as they worked really hard to drop deeply into their pre-performance routines. Given they would also have a powerful Pathway 1 philosophy, they would be feeling courage and they would have a deep belief in their skill, and the determination and discipline to stick to their plan. Deep down, they would have complete acceptance that they may lose or fail, and that is OK.

I often talk about the 'Novak Djokovic moment', which refers to the US Open in 2011 when Roger Federer had two match points against Novak in the semi-final. Djokovic was up against what most people would believe to be insurmountable odds. He was two match points down, playing against the greatest tennis player ever. He was also in front of tens of thousands of spectators and possibly hundreds of millions of television viewers all around the world. The difference between winning and losing the next point was over a million dollars in winnings!

Now, in most circumstances, athletes become inhibited under such pressure, or repress rather than express themselves. Not Novak – he expressed himself completely and unleashed his mind, hitting a beautiful forehand winner that turned the tide in the game. He subsequently broke Federer's serve and went on to win the match! This example highlights the absolute world-class nature of his underlying success rules, and it was not the first or only time he expressed himself so fully under such pressure. For him to do so, he must have expressive success rules that target how he does what he does, and are not limited by outcome or results. For example: success equals failing from a strong place; success equals hitting the ball hard; success equals courage to just play; success equals expressing myself; success equals stepping in and embracing pressure; success equals going for it and having fun!

Because the 12 non-outcome success rules listed above are process rules, they are automatically true Pathway 1 success rules. Remember, Pathway 1 is about process; it is about how we apply ourselves to what we are doing, rather than getting caught up in or locked in to the outcome. Pathway 1 and its success rules reflect a deep trust that if you focus on the process the outcome will take care of itself. Following Pathway 1 success rules will always leave you feeling strangely calm, and as though you can't fail. That is how you know when you have nailed the correct rules!

When watching sport, it is easy to pick the athletes with strong process or Pathway 1 success rules. They seem to seldom think about outcome, even when winning. They are most preoccupied with understanding various mechanical elements of their sport. When hearing them talk after a great performance, or even a terrible one, they seem more excited about a revelation they may have had about a part of their game than the result. When you see an athlete like this take note because if they are any good skill-wise, I would expect them to go a very long way! Their behaviour tells us that they see success as expressing themselves and learning rather than a score or outcome. This sort of mindset is absolute gold!

'SUCCESS RULES' IS PERHAPS THE MOST RADICAL DISCUSSION YOU WILL HAVE WITH YOURSELF

Establishing non-outcome success rules is radical thinking! Often, when I have these discussions with athletes, they think I am saying that they should not care about outcome. They also feel afraid that I am trying to make them lazy because they think I am getting them to take the demand to work hard off them. Their deeper belief is that if they do not focus on outcome they will have nothing to motivate themselves. Further, they also hold on very strongly to the idea that sport is all about outcome and winning.

They could not be more wrong! Sport is about pitting yourself against yourself, and expressing yourself under pressure and challenge. It is about stepping into the challenge competition throws at you and not backing away from it to try to protect your score or the outcome. Ironically, in the end, sport is in no way about the score. The score, just like your bank account in life, when it is all said and done, means very little indeed!

It is important to stress that by suggesting you establish powerful helpful success rules like the ones discussed in this section, I am not trying to undermine your mental toughness; rather, I am adding to it. When athletes have helpful, powerful success rules and follow Pathway 1 values of hard work, planning, courage and patience, they not only remain competitive and love winning, but the urge to follow their rules grows at the unconscious level and becomes like an unlimited source of energy and motivation. Further, they free themselves up mentally and lose the previous polluting need to win, score well and perform perfectly. They drop into another universe where they work even harder and with greater intensity than they ever thought was possible. They realise really quickly that they still want to have great outcomes, but they no longer feel the stress of 'needing to' or 'having to' perform well.

The shift from having to to wanting to perform is massive! It is the same as moving from obsessive-compulsive traits in practice and performance, where athletes feel 'driven' to practise and feel that they must perform well, to practising and performing for the love of it. When an athlete feels passionate about practice and performing, it is so much easier on their spirit and mind; they become much more relaxed and free. Practice and performing become things that nurture their soul and spirit, unleashing a boundless energy and enthusiasm to do more!

Here is a powerful example of what can happen when an entire team lets go of outcome pressure and moves from feeling like they have to perform to not caring at all about results and being driven more by their connection with each other and the love of just 'going for it'. In 2012, the Waikato Bay of Plenty Magic netball team was four losses from four games and sitting 10th on the Championship table. The team was filled with world-class players, but they were just not 'clicking'. They were struggling to let go and simply play. Once they lost the first four games, they were forced into a corner of having to 'go for it' or be doomed. The result in shifting from outcome thinking to a 'who cares, let's just play' mindset was remarkable. Here is a great reflection from the coach on what she saw happen in the 2012 Championship winning year.

THE 'MAGIC' FROM DROPPING DEEPLY INTO NON-OUTCOME SUCCESS RULES

Our transition from being 10th on the table after four consecutive losses in the first four rounds to winning 12 straight games in a row and being crowned ANZ Champions 2012 was not an easy feat. The golden key in our transition was to let go of outcome focus and reach a place that only few people talk about ever achieving: a place of deep respect, trust and love for each other, and surrender of outcome; a place where only the team matters and you know others have your back no matter what. For the last five weeks of the competition, I believe we were in the 'zone'. Nothing else mattered apart from each other. Ironically, when we were in this deep place, there was a kind of sense or knowingness that we were never going to lose. It was just amazing to be a part of. At the end it wasn't about the win, it was more about the journey and the emotional roller coaster ride that we all had to endure that filled us with the greatest sense of achievement and pride. The level of vulnerability that is required to enter into this space, coupled with the determination, drive and passion to succeed, is a beautiful balance of ingredients that produces moments of magic.

Noeline Taurua

In early 2012 the team launched its new dress design. It represents Mahuika, Maori goddess of fire, and the mountain, sea and lakes of the Waikato and Bay of Plenty regions. The team walked to the top of Mount Maunganui to bless the uniform at the arrival of the dawn. This forging of the team unity meant that, under the pressure of losing the first four games of the 2012 season, they could trust in each other, let go of any outcome fears and come together as one to just unleash!

INCORPORATING YOUR NEW SUCCESS RULES INTO YOUR PRACTICE AND PLAY

Establishing powerful success rules will pay immediate dividends in your levels of self-belief, confidence and enthusiasm to practise and perform. It will give you a new way to support your thinking and talking to ensure you continue growing self-belief and confidence during success, adversity and failing.

Ask yourself the following simple question when reviewing a performance both during and afterwards, to inject your new success rules into your performances:

How was I successful today (first set, half, second set, half, etc)?

Make sure you ask this question irrespective of whether you performed well or poorly, won or lost.

Now look at how you achieved your success rules (e.g. 'had fun' or 'went for it' if your success rules are 'success equals fun' and 'go for it'). Notice how this makes you feel. Even if you performed badly, focusing your mind in this way will help you feel more of a success than a failure.

Later in the book, I will discuss performance language. This is a simple language base to help focus your mind into Pathway 1 and MOP universe. 'How was I successful today?' is a performance language question. Here are three other simple questions you could use to help incorporate your new success rules into your practice and performance reviewing:

What was my best memory from today when I _____?
(Put success rule in here; e.g. unleashed the beast)

What was one thing I learnt today that will help me _____ next time I practise and play? (e.g. unleash the beast)

What was I most proud of today when I _____?
(e.g. unleashed the beast)

Look for situations when before you may have folded under pressure, but now are learning to embrace and unleash in them.

You should build your responses initially on paper so you can 'learn' how they should sound when you talk to yourself, others or even the media.

Here are a couple of complete example answers to the question below to reinforce how your answers need to start sounding in your mind and in discussions with your key support people (e.g. coach) and the media:

How was I successful today?

> **Success rule (tennis): have courage to stick to the game plan**
>
> One way I was really successful today was sticking to my game plan. Not once did I adjust my approach. I followed the plan in every game and across every set. It felt great to approach each point with such confidence and certainty!
>
> **Success rule (golf): putt strongly along the line**
>
> One way I was really successful today was with my putting. I putted strongly along the line all day. I found my pre-putt routine was robust under pressure. I had a great view of the line and then pure intention to putt along it. The stuff we are working on really helped my mind. It has never felt so strong, so pure, so unpolluted by negative thinking. I was alive!

Initially you will need to ask yourself the full questions. However, as you become more familiar with this mindset you will be able to initiate this thinking by simply asking yourself, 'How was my _____ today?' (e.g. golf). You should then be able to reply with a variety of statements, such as, 'One way I was successful today was _____.' When this occurs, you will know that you are developing a powerful automatic mindset.

BUILDING POWERFUL NON-OUTCOME SUCCESS RULES: EXERCISE 4

Establishing Powerful Answers to Your Evolving Success Rules

Take some time to prepare standard answers to the following questions using your success rules. Your answers should have as much detail as my example responses in the box above.

How was my _____ today?

How was I successful today?

When you have completed your model answers, identify two opportunities when you can next inject your new success rules into your language. For example, when you next review with your coach or parents.

In summary, establishing powerful success rules that have nothing to do with outcome itself, and everything to do with the process of performing, is perhaps the most vital work you will undertake when programming your mind for success! Doing this well will take time and discipline. You need to teach your mind what success looks like so you can unlock your deep playing potential and perform with a free spirit and from instinct like Novak Djokovic.

Make no mistake: if you have success rules that are linked to outcome, you are in for a rough ride. One day, you will feel like you can take on the world and win major championships, and the very next you may feel like the worst athlete on the planet. Linking success to outcome guarantees that your emotions will be up and down depending on the results and where you finish in an event: euphoric one day, depressed the next; excited and happy one minute, angry and frustrated the next; confident and self-believing one moment, ripped apart by self-doubt the next.

Powerful, helpful success rules that are linked to non-outcome processes (i.e. how you do what you do) set an athlete up to feel successful, even when they are failing and going through adversity. Achieve strong non-outcome success rules and observe how a deep maturity establishes in you and your performance. Further, develop non-outcome success rules and notice how, when you do fail, it seems to have little impact on you whatsoever. This resilience will be a result of you developing deeper self-acceptance. As a result of this emotional development, you will be very calm under pressure and almost serene in contexts where outcome-driven or obsessed people fall apart. Over time, your emotions will remain constant and stable because they are directly related to the process and things you have complete control over. That is, when you link success to how you behave, you can guarantee you will feel successful!

MOMENTS OF PERFECTION: MOP UNIVERSE!

In addition to building powerful non-outcome success rules, perhaps the other most powerful aspect of the Pathway 1 philosophy is MOP universe. In essence, MOP universe is where a person focuses on what is working and any example (a Moment of Perfection) of moving in the right direction towards a desired outcome. Many people I speak with hold to the belief that perfection is impossible and asking athletes to focus on MOPs and hunt for them is unhelpful and even damaging, as it sets them up for failure. They tell me that perfectionism is destructive to a person's confidence and self-belief, and suffocates ambition. I couldn't disagree more!

When I worked as a traditional psychologist with people with depression and anxiety, I often heard them say, 'The reason I am so unhappy or worried is that I am a perfectionist.' They would proceed to tell me about everything that was going wrong in their lives and their main character flaws. It was then that I would always stop them and ask, 'If you are so much of a perfectionist, why are you telling me about all the negative stuff, or the sh*t?' I would tell them that they were not perfectionists at all, and in fact were 'imperfectionists' as all they focused on and talked about were examples of imperfection.

They would get it and smile. I would then have them live to their perfectionist title and tell me all about what was working in their lives and what their strengths were. Surprise, surprise, they would start to feel better and have higher hopes than when they came in, just from doing that. The first homework they would get from me was to record all the good things that happened across their week (i.e. the MOP book). By the following session, they were always feeling better!

MOP UNIVERSE: EXERCISE 1

What Are You – a Perfectionist or an Imperfectionist?

Prove it! Write a summary of your week up to now. Write non-stop for one minute about the week without thinking about it. Just write down whatever comes to mind about the things that happened. For example:
1. I was late to the meeting with Peter.
2. Jane made a critical comment about my dress.

Write your summary here:

_____
_____
_____
_____
_____
_____

Look at the themes or trends in your summary. Are you focusing on Moments of Perfection or Moments of Sh*t? Write some notes to yourself here based on whether you are a perfectionist or imperfectionist.

Moments of Perfection occur all the time and they are incredibly powerful for growing self-belief and confidence, then enthusiasm and ambition. Sadly, most people choose not to notice them. We seem locked in to focusing on error due to what appears to be a deeply held belief, in New Zealand anyway, that we learn best through trial and error, or Moments of Sh*t.

PERFECTION EXISTS AND OCCURS FREQUENTLY

My daughter's smile is perfect, every time! The sunrise is perfect every time because it means I am alive; sometimes it is even more perfect than at other times because I am doing things I really enjoy. Waking up healthy is perfect. Often athletes make an execution so precise it sounds perfect, shapes perfectly onto the target, or hits exactly where it was intended. Athletes gripped by fear of failing who choose to face that fear down and unleash their minds anyway are perfect. Trusting in your practice and skill and not caring about the outcome because it is more important to you to act from courage and go for it than to give in to fear is another example of perfection.

I choose to live in MOP universe. Every person, from a lawn bowler to a priest, makes a choice every moment whether to live in MOP universe or not. To live in MOP universe is easy when everything is going well and you are winning or performing really well. The true test of your mind's default is to look at whether you are focusing on Moments of Perfection or Moments of Sh*t when adversity strikes and you are 'failing' miserably; for example, if the media writes only about how terrible you are. The perfect place to be is MOP universe when you are failing and/or under pressure. To be focused on Moments of Perfection when everyone else is focused on Moments of Shi*t is truly MOP universe!

THE ESSENCE OF MOP UNIVERSE

Athletes and other people living in MOP universe look for, focus on and internalise any piece of evidence, no matter how big or small, that proves that their strategic plan is working and they will achieve their Impossible Dream. Moments of Perfection include external outcome results as well as internal process evidence. For example, a player in golf may nail a drive down a hole that has previously scared them. This is a great MOP and evidence that their plan to grow courage, mental toughness and play from Pathway 1 is working. That same player may then three-putt the green on the same hole, but come away feeling successful because they hit their putts strong along the line they intended the ball to go in the first place. Their courage and commitment to their putting routine was a massive MOP, as too was their mindset when reflecting on and reviewing their hole from MOP universe after making bogey. Living MOPs purely and from full Pathway 1 will generate great confidence and self-belief, and result in a feeling more satisfying than the buzz associated with any outcome. Here is a short passage from Olympic silver medallist BMX rider Sarah Walker, highlighting the power of MOP universe to help her grow confidence and self-belief, and live from courage. Sarah found that having fun on (and off) her bike was critical to her robust confidence leading up to the London games. MOP universe was perfect for that!

THE POWER OF MOP UNIVERSE AND HAVING FUN DOING WHAT YOU DO

MOP universe helped me start to believe in myself and grow my self-confidence. Finding those things that made me proud every day allowed me to smile about what I was doing and grow a positive mindset rather than a negative one. In a sport like BMX, where confidence can make a huge difference in the way we ride our bikes, MOP universe allowed me to grow that confidence to the point where I was doing things I had never tried before.

I will never be 'fearless.' But I have learnt how to live and ride from courage. By focusing on the process and visualising my success before I attempt something that scares me, I can put that fear and doubt to the side while I drop into Pathway 1 and do what I need to do to be my absolute best. MOP universe has been a critical element to me achieving that skill.

Sarah Walker

LIVING IN PURE MOP UNIVERSE – CHALLENGING TRADITIONAL LOCK-INS FOR HOW THE WORLD SHOULD LOOK

I am a MOP extremist! I live, breath and eat MOPs. I spend hours thinking about how MOP universe looks and works in high-performance sport. I spend just as many hours training my children in MOP universe so that by the time they reach secondary school it will be their primary default. **Living in true MOP universe within the Pathway 1 framework outlined in this book (e.g. detail and planning, crystal-clear targets, and weekly and daily plans) removes the need to ever look at a mistake or MOS again.** This is because working hard to a clear, detailed and accurate plan will lead to improvement without even having to think about it.

This is a pretty extreme statement and one that certainly gets a lot of challenge from coaches, parents and teachers. When I make this claim, most people tell me it is just not possible to live that way. People seem to struggle with MOP universe because, as I mentioned earlier, our dominant 'lock-in' is that we learn best through error, failing and/or adversity. Further, common practice in schools and with coaches reflects a deep, ingrained belief that we must immerse ourselves in Moments of Sh*t to make sure we get the message and learn our lesson. It is as though not looking at our errors and mistakes leaves people feeling uncomfortable or uneasy. It seems that their discomfort is based on a fear that they will not learn, and that the mistakes will occur again. That is, their primary purpose is to avoid mistakes and failing. This mindset is the core driver in Pathway 2 and is the opposite to Pathway 1. People living by Pathway 1 are primarily motivated by wanting to nail the process, to win, to get things right, to be perfect and to obtain excellence, never to avoid things going wrong.

I try to explain to people that trial and error learning (i.e. learning from each MOS) is possible and can work, but that it is slow and psychologically painful. There is a scientifically proven law in psychology: What we pay attention to increases the probability that very thing we focus on will occur again (i.e. by looking at errors we unwittingly increase the probability that they will occur again). This is much like when one pays attention to a little child's temper tantrums – it actually increases the probability they will continue to have them. Even though eventually errors do reduce, it takes far more work to get to that point than it does by focusing on MOPs.

Many people look at me in a strange way when I mention this law of psychology, then they quickly discount me and my ideas. It seems that their own lock-ins prevent them from being open-minded to other possibilities of learning and growth. It is as though they have a fixed or closed mindset. They are closing their minds off to an entirely different universe or source of potential without even experimenting with it or giving it a try for a period of time. Unfortunately, these people are closing themselves off from something very special.

Here is an example of just how powerful MOP universe can be. The next passage is from World Cup-winning All Black Richard Kahui. He and Stephen Donald were great guinea pigs of mine when working with the Chiefs. They were always keen to try the next little thing to come to my mind, such as MOP universe, which had a massive positive impact on Richard.

THE POWER OF MOP UNIVERSE

It was 2010, and I must have been the worst player in the world (at least that's what my head was telling me). I was right in the middle of Pathway 2. This came about because I was coming back from injury and I'd had a couple of average games in a row. Then I had a nightmare of a game, dropping maybe five balls, but worse, trying not to go anywhere near the ball for fear of making a mistake and even changing the calls so I didn't have to touch it. I was so negative about making mistakes, and what people would think, and if the ABs' coaches were watching, so I froze. I was in

Richard in full flight against the French in the 2011 Rugby World Cup final: another MOP!

the middle of Pathway 2 with no way out.

I was in a bad place mentally until I sat down with DG and started to talk pathways, and it became obvious I was not living Pathway 1 – I was not even close. We talked about what Pathway 1 looks like and what it means to live Pathway 1 and live in a MOP universe. DG and I worked closely over the next month with a real MOP focus, looking at my MOPs and growing my self-belief and understanding.

There was a particular moment during a game when it all hit me and I thought: *F__ it!* What that meant to me was that I was ready to live Pathway 1 and challenge myself to perfection, live without fear of failure, live in the now, believe that I could be the best in the world and back my ability. It changed my footy and my life. It took over my way of thinking and, more importantly, the way I did things. I started playing like a world-beater, made the ABs and went on to play well at international level. Sure, I still had moments of self-doubt and Pathway 2, but I had the mental skills to get me back on Pathway 1. These skills and living in a MOP universe carried me all the way to winning the Rugby World Cup in 2011, and are skills I use in my everyday life.

Kaks

MOP UNIVERSE: EXERCISE 2

Is Your Mind MOP or MOS Dominant?

It is quite easy to find out if you focus more on Moments of Perfection or Moments of Sh*t in your life. All you need to do is to record how much time your mind focuses on each during the time you perform, practise and train. This will give you your MOP to MOS ratio.

A person who is MOP dominant spends far more time reminiscing on what went well and enjoying memories of when they performed well.

A person who is MOS dominant spends far more time ruminating over what went wrong and where they could improve. They often fantasise in their mind and rerun various mistakes in order to almost rescript what actually happened.

In your next practice session or round record:

The number of times I caught myself focusing on a MOP _____

The number of times I caught myself focusing on a MOS _____

Reflect on how you were feeling when you were either MOS or MOP dominant. Which did it feel best to focus on? In which universe did you feel you could perform your best and get the most enjoyment from your pursuit?

Write a few thoughts here for yourself on whether you would like to be more MOP dominant and how you could do this.

MOP Versus MOS Coaching Paradigm – a Real-Life Example

When discussing MOP universe with coaches, I share the following story with them to help them see what I am talking about and the possibility that there are other ways to learn and grow.

When my second daughter was four years old, we decided it was time to prepare her for school and for her to learn to write. At the time, I was starting to reflect on MOP universe. I took the opportunity to experiment with the impact of MOP and MOS universes on her confidence and self-belief, and subsequent ability to learn handwriting.

We printed off everything we needed. On day one, I decided to run MOS universe only, focusing on and commenting only on the things she did wrong. When my daughter got up to the table for her first 'lesson' she was full of confidence; she had learnt to hold the pencil correctly and was drawing nicely given her age.

She started with 'a'. She made her first mistake at the very point she put her pencil to paper, missing the starting mark. I stopped her immediately and said, 'That is not where we start; that is wrong. We start here. Do it again.'

Straight away, her arms and face tensed up. She was now nervous and fearful. She had performance anxiety! She made the same mistake again, which I let go because I couldn't bring myself to be so extreme MOS, and I knew another mistake would not be far away. As she came around the bottom of the 'a' she missed connecting the base of it with the line. It was her second mistake in less than 10 seconds! I stopped her again and told her that she had

Grace fishing in the central North Island of New Zealand, aged six years old.

made another mistake and that was not how you do the bottom of the 'a'. She stopped, dropped the pencil onto the table, and got up and left without making a sound. She walked quickly into the lounge and found her blanket.

We have four blankets strategically placed around the family home as they are that important to her. She started to self-soothe by rubbing the corner of the blanket under her nose. She was crying. With two comments, I had shattered my daughter's confidence and belief in herself, so much so that she was in tears and refused to come back to the table because I had made learning to write painful. In psychology-speak I had generated an aversion response in two events!

Human emotions do not grow older as we grow older. Emotions are ageless. When a child feels emotions (e.g. performance anxiety and embarrassment or shame) it is absolutely pure. It exists unpolluted by adult social conditioning about how we are expected to feel and express our emotions. For example, when a three year old feels grief, it is infinitely powerful. When a 34 year old feels grief, it is exactly the same emotion, only now it is repressed and tempered by social conditioning. It has become less consciously sharp and acute by the lessons we have learnt across our lifetime about *how* one should experience and express grief.

This reflection becomes important when considering the psychological process my daughter went through during her first MOS handwriting lesson at my school of hard knocks. The following diagram shows what happens psychologically in the MOS universe and what occurred rapidly for Grace. The cycle starts with the MOS: her first mistake with her pencil.

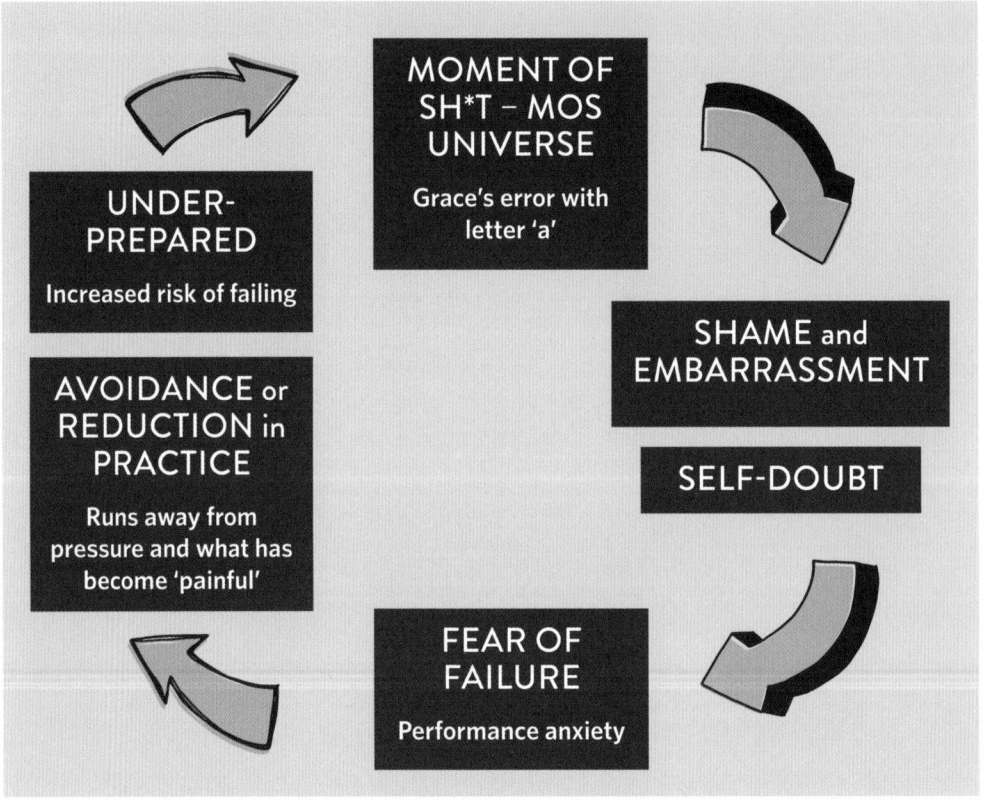

The MOS universe cycle of shame starts with the Moment of Sh*t at the top of the diagram.

When I highlighted my daughter's failing to her, she went very quickly through this shame or MOS cycle. The first time it impacted on her confidence and self-belief, but she managed to hold it together and try again for her daddy. The second time I highlighted her error, however, it was too much for her little mind and she collapsed under the pressure and sought to escape from a situation that had very quickly become emotionally painful. Over time, had I continued down this road with her, it would have created a fixed neural pattern or 'wired-in' habit of avoiding pressure and risk of failing (i.e. learning situations). Imagine the impact that would have had on her transition into school!

Make no mistake, this happens a lot in our children. Most behavioural problems in young children at school are due to 'learning' becoming painful because they feel that they are failing. Their bad behaviour is an escape or way of getting out of the pain. Teenagers and adults are no different. Their feelings related to failing are just as powerful. Those who say being told that what they do wrong does not affect them are lying! It does affect them. All that is different between them and my daughter is they have learnt that they must or should be open to feedback and learn through their mistakes. That they must 'suck it up' and take it. Unfortunately, our unconscious mind does not follow the same rules, and with every mistake or bit of negative feedback, there will be a resulting increase in self-doubt and a drop in confidence. What usually happens is that adults take MOS-based feedback for a period of time and then start to avoid the situation. Just like my little Grace, it becomes too much for them to handle, and they want to leave and often not come back.

In sport, a dominant MOS-universe mindset may be reflected in an athlete talking about how they have lost their love of the game or even that they have started to hate what they used to love. They may start arriving late, avoiding the coach or missing appointments, testing and video sessions. They are mostly likely aware of a drop in confidence, an increase in self-doubt and a lack of desire or enthusiasm to practise (refer back to diagram above).

This is all a direct result of living in MOS universe.

Back to my story about Grace: I spent the rest of the day playing dollies with my daughter in order to make things OK between us again, and for Dad to feel less stink after smashing her confidence. Fortunately, children are incredibly forgiving and before long she was laughing and smiling again.

Day two brought session two of my little mind experiment. The difficulty I had getting my daughter to come back to the table for her second lesson in handwriting shows just how quickly children (and adolescents and adults) lose confidence and unconsciously want to avoid experiences or situations that they associate with embarrassment, shame or emotional pain. In order to get her back to the table I had to bribe her with chocolate buttons. I told my daughter that today the rules had changed, that she would be able to earn chocolate buttons for her effort. She loves chocolate buttons, so she came back. We were underway again!

She made the same mistake that she'd made the first day. So she had not learnt through trial and error. I ignored it. She then made the same mistake on the bottom of the 'a'. I ignored that too. The back of her 'a' was almost perfect. I stopped her, and she froze. She was waiting for me to tell her it was wrong! I said to her, 'That is the best back of an 'a' that I have ever seen, and that is worth five chocolate buttons.' I also said that she could eat them one by one or all at once. As you can guess, she ate them all at once! Her learning took off like a space rocket at hyper-speed. We were off!

At the time of writing this book, my daughter is seven years old. She has been writing for approximately three years and her handwriting is better than most 12-year-olds.

Never again did I stop her on a handwriting MOS. I have only ever commented on her MOPs, and we have done all our learning on how to write through MOP universe. **Perhaps the greatest gift that this process has given her is an enormous appetite for learning and a wonderful enjoyment for school.** She loves school more than being at home and cries when the school holidays come around! As far as I am concerned, if all athletes or coaches reject MOP universe I do not care because it has given my children and me as a dad a wonderful, enriching gift!

It would be sad, however, if coaches and players did not experiment with MOP universe because they would miss an opportunity to unleash possibly the greatest learning and performance tool. Imagine if your children and athletes evolved the same spirited appetite for learning that little Grace has. The diagram below shows the MOP cycle, which is just as powerful as the MOS cycle shown above only this one is emotionally positive. Instead of feeding self-doubt and fear of failure, it grows pride, self-belief, confidence and enthusiasm to do more practice.

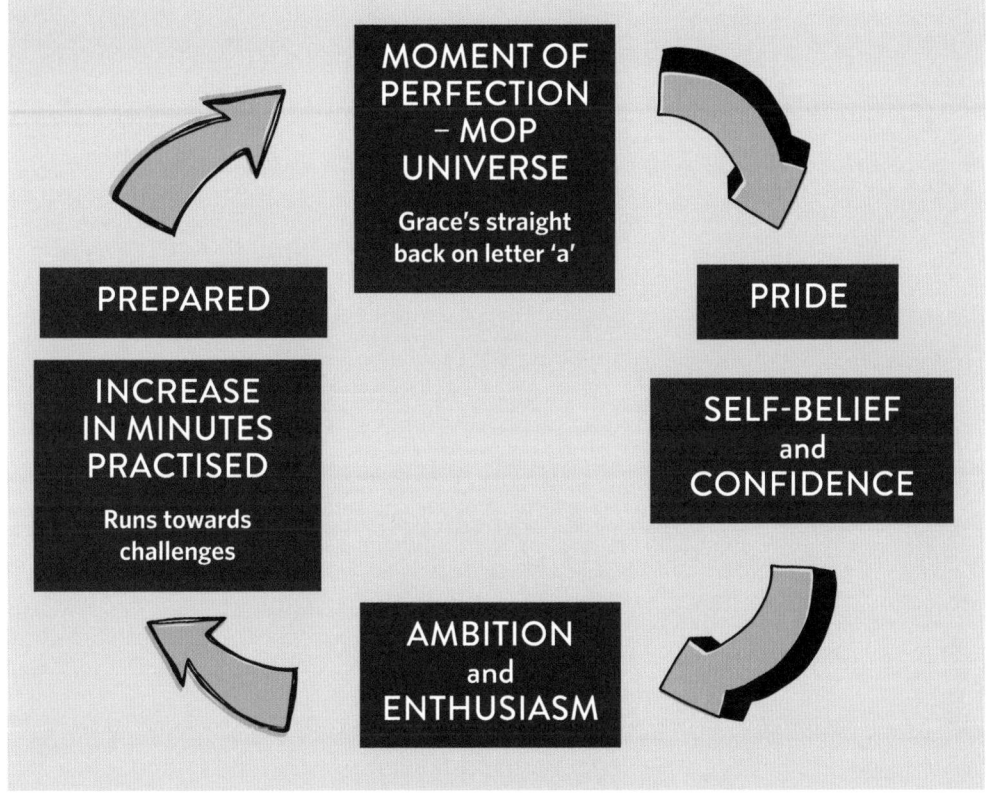

The MOP universe cycle of pride starts with the Moment of Perfection at the top of the diagram.

When you see and speak with athletes and people locked in the MOP cycle, you are left with an impression that they absolutely love life and their sport. Their passion is overwhelming and their work ethic inspiring. Their ambition skyrockets and they become absolutely committed to mastering what they do. Athletes and coaches find their sessions and interactions an absolute joy and totally pure. This is all because of MOP universe!

MOP Universe in Action – the Key Points

1. **It is important to note that focusing on MOPs and learning through them is only part of the equation for optimal development.** All the components discussed in this book are critical to enable yourself to fully live in MOP universe. For example, it is impossible to live in MOP universe if your success rule is 'Don't make mistakes!' Living from this sort of success rule will drive you into MOS universe.

   Further, it is absolutely critical you have a long-term plan with in-depth, vivid and objective details about the end point in order to facilitate unconscious growth and movement towards that point. This will unconsciously drive you to notice the MOPs that are the most important and relevant to the end point, and thereby speed up your development.

   Living in MOP universe speeds up the unconscious drive to get to the dream because it fuels the fire. By itself, MOP universe surpasses learning through MOS universe. It will not on its own, however, fully tap into or unleash the deep infinite power inside; we need all the Pathway 1 ingredients for that to happen.

2. **Living in MOP universe is not all roses and marshmallows.** Often athletes and coaches misinterpret MOP universe as being the easy road, when in fact most people find living in genuine MOP universe too hard and find MOS universe much easier. MOS universe only requires that you focus on Moments of Sh*t from the last performance and then try to fix them in time to perform at the next one. MOS universe is locked into

this week, and the here and now, driven from Pathway 2 fear of failure. For MOP universe to be most effective, it needs to be based on a foundation of detailed planning and homework (i.e. strategic plans for the coming season or year and looking forward many years – five, ten or even fifteen). Living from this philosophy involves massive commitment to mastering the game.

3. **Living in MOP universe requires a regular formal review, which demands absolute ruthless personal accountability; it is the polar opposite of 'marshmallow world'!** Ideally you should hold a formal review every week. Some athletes prefer to do them more regularly, especially if they are training or practising many hours a day. Essentially it is up to you. If you find yourself doing them too often, however, it could be a sign that you are seeking reassurance that you are still on track (Pathway 2), or that you are actually living in MOS universe and are using the formal review to punish yourself for mistakes.

    You drive the formal review, getting feedback from the key people on your team (e.g. coach, parent, bio mechanist, etc). The review is driven using the following question format:

    How good am I at: skill A, skill B, skill C, etc?

For example, in golf: How good am I at fairways in regulation?
    A rating out of 10 should be reached after getting feedback from all the people involved in the review. A rating of 10/10 mean you are good enough to achieve a specific target on your plan (e.g. to qualify for the OneAsia tour) rather than the final destination (e.g. to be world number one) unless that is where your development is at. Data should also consulted, if available, to help generate an objective rating.
    The rating may be 0/10. Now that is brutal! It is important that you are able to ask the key question above without making excuses, using any give-up talk or seeking

reassurance. Low ratings will make your tummy go tight and you will get uncomfortable. If you can hold on to this discomfort without using excuses, you will grow mentally tougher and get to a point where 'failing' will no longer have an emotional impact on you. Imagine the freedom that will come with that! You will then find yourself performing from a pure mindset where you no longer try to either make things happen or avoid things happening; you will just perform. Paradise! Further, you will start to find that you react less to bad outcomes (e.g. hitting the ball over the base line in a critical rally) or 'unlucky breaks' during a game.

Formal strategic plans to success should only ever be adjusted based on formal data and feedback, never on a hunch or a feeling. This is another reason why formal reviews are so important, and why stats over a long period of time (i.e. at least three to six months) should be used wherever possible when making significant changes to your plan.

4. **Outside of the formal reviews, only MOP feedback is permitted.** For example, in rugby the coach most often blows the whistle when a MOS occurs. They pull all the players in to discuss the MOS in great detail, and then rerun the drill. Often the coach does not comment once on the many MOPs that occurred before the MOS! In MOP universe, the opposite occurs. You do not comment on a MOS; you ignore it! You focus on, think about and talk about MOPs. You discuss these with your coach and ensure you have a deep understanding about how each one happened, thereby learning the mechanics of what you need to do through success not failing. Imagine that – an environment where the coach never comments on or stops play for mistakes. You can see why most coaches laugh at me when I talk about MOP universe; they genuinely think I am mad!

5. **MOP universe has its own language: performance language.** I have put a performance language sheet in the appendix for you to use to build your own performance

language structure that you will utilise when discussing your sport or other pursuit with anyone (e.g. your partner, your parents or your coach). MOP performance language supports a person to have optimistic thinking and perception about all events. The greatest reward of performance language is that it assists you to succeed and fail strong. Using the language helps you continue to grow self-belief and confidence, no matter what the outcome of your event, training or practice. Here is an example of how I have used performance language with my two daughters to highlight the massive impact it has on a person psychologically.

THE POWER OF MOP UNIVERSE PERFORMANCE LANGUAGE

Since my daughters were five and seven years old, they have been 'trained' in using performance language, and they did not even know it. When I picked them up from school, I would ask the following specific questions:

What was your best memory today at school?

What did you learn at school today that will help you tomorrow or later in life?

What were you most proud about from today?

When discussing with my children what pride means, they came up with a fantastic definition. Pride to them is being happy with how they behaved. Pretty neat definition!

I would often ask the questions while eating a nice afternoon tea or drinking a hot chocolate drink, thereby further increasing the 'feel-good' associations with thinking and talking this way, and locking them in to their young, open minds.

After a time, when the girls got used to doing the reviews, I started to ask who would go first. They would race to say, 'I am

Two pretty cool kids, day's end, Whakapapa ski field.

first.' Then it progressed further, and they started to race to me in the school ground to say they would be first with their reviews.

It took off to a place I had never imagined it would go. They started to review spontaneously during the day, and up to 15 times across the day they would yell, 'I am first,' with no cue from me. They started to talk to each other within this framework as they went about their day-to-day lives at home. It became their language – normal and instinctive. They did not have to force themselves to think like this; it became their minds' natural way of doing it.

My goal had been to have them conditioned by the time they were 10 to 15 years old, so that if they played sport, they would have powerful mental toughness, and no matter how they performed they would base their thinking around the same questions above. They were way ahead of what I had planned.

Imagine how you would feel asking yourself those questions as you reviewed how you were playing during an event (e.g. between points in tennis or halves in soccer). The feedback from athletes thinking this way is incredibly positive.

I deeply believe that my daughters thinking this way, and MOP universe in general, has had a massive positive impact on their evolving minds and personalities.

MOP UNIVERSE: EXERCISE 2

Designing Your Own Performance Language Framework

Now it is time to design your own performance language framework. Go to Appendix 1 – Performance Language – and read through the various questions. Choose three or four key questions that your mind likes the sound of, and write them in here.

Performance language critical questions:

1. _____
2. _____
3. _____
4. _____

Once you have decided on your questions, sit down with your coach, parent(s) and partner or key friends supporting you and discuss MOP universe and performance language with them. Make sure they understand that this is the language you are now going to live and play by and that, from that moment forward, whenever they ask you how something went, you will use your key language to review and answer.

For example, if you choose the same questions my daughters use, your answers may sound like this:

1. **My best memory** today was my drive down 15 (golf). I was petrified of going OB, but not once did I back down. I injected courage and played right along the OB line, just like I had planned to and how the hole was designed to be played.

2. **I learnt** that when I picture the LION in my mind before I serve the ball (tennis), and then have a deep, quiet 'standing still thinking nothing' moment, I seem to stop thinking and drop into instinct mode. After that, the shot takes care of itself! It is beautiful. I must keep working on mastering how to inject the LION when I want to, and being able to achieve deep instinct within a breath or two.
3. **I was most proud of** my preparation leading up to my game today. I have been steadily getting better and better at paying the price with my training during the week, and it feels as though today's performance is a direct result of how many minutes I am now committing to in the key areas of my game. It feels great!

Responding to MOS Universe Thinking and Talking

Make sure that your parent(s), coach or others supporting you read over the entire Appendix 1 as there is a very important bit at the end outlining how they are to deal with you when you do not use MOP performance language and start using MOS-based language (usually after a bad outcome). For example, if you start talking about all the things that went wrong or how you performed badly (i.e. how most athletes talk after failing!) The key is for them not to get hooked in to the discussion with you. If you start MOS thinking, all they need to say to you is:

> **'It does not look like you are ready for us to review your performance. I am going to have a coffee. Let me know when you are ready to use the questions and language we have decided to use, and we can talk.'**

The greatest benefit of using this method is that your support people do not have to be your psychologist. When you have to work hard to think with a MOP mindset and then come back ready to talk to your support people, your mind grows stronger and more robust. The more you can switch back from MOS to MOP thinking and have your support people use MOP performance language, the easier it will be for you to live in MOP universe when performing, training and practising, even when things are going badly.

6. **Make yourself keep a MOP book and record notes in it at training, practice and during performances, if possible.**
   For example, you could write in it after each shot in golf, or in between change of ends in tennis. I want this to become a key success maker for you, or something that over time you start to see as being critical to your performance success. Buy the cheapest little notebook, it does not have to be expensive. Exercise 3 below uses a golf example to show how you can use the MOP book.

MOP UNIVERSE: EXERCISE 3

Using a MOP Book

Whenever you have a MOP (e.g. a beautiful, soft, high seven iron fade), simply record it in your MOP book as you walk down the fairway (in golf).

Entry example 1 for a MOP outcome:

Hole 14: beautiful, sweet, soft, high seven iron to six feet! Mint!

A MOP does not have to be an outcome, it can be a process or it can be based on your feelings and how you played.

Entry example 2 for a MOP process:

Hole 1: 40 people watching me tee off, really nervous, used Pathway 1 and injected the LION, which anchored me in courage and felt really calm when addressing ball. Outstanding!

The following is a review from a promising young amateur golfer, Dave Feeney, who has really grabbed the MOP book idea and run with it.

THE POWER OF THE MOP BOOK

In my opinion, the MOP book that you suggested has been the most valuable asset you have given me. As of late 2013, I have tested the MOP book's effectiveness on the course through 18 holes. Using the MOP book on EVERY hole for at least one shot, or even a positive or happy thought, has made me focus only on the positives in my game and life.

Without the MOP book through the 18 holes I had struggled to control my emotions. Some examples of this would be swearing, banging clubs on the ground, getting frustrated at my playing partners and just having an all-round negative outlook on the game.

Also, after doing the MOP book at the end of the round, good or bad, I come off feeling positive. I still go through the round and debrief on some mistakes that need fixing, but I don't sulk after a bad game any more.

In my opinion, people who have been told to do the MOP book and haven't tried it SHOULD! It could be the one thing, that one

Another one for the MOP book! Dave practises in Auckland, New Zealand.

weapon that you need to break through and dominate. I'll be using the MOP book till the day I die, and when I make it to world number one! The MOP book will be one of the huge factors in my success.

MOP!

David Feeney

In summary, MOP universe is a complete revolution in the way you approach how you think and talk about sport and life, no matter what you are pursuing. Gone are the days of sitting around thinking about how unlucky you are and all those 'putts that did not drop'. From now on, you are going to sound so different from everyone else that they will probably tell you to go and see a psychologist because you must be insane! That is when you can give them my card and tell them you are seeing a psychologist already and that it is the best thing you ever did.

Fully committing to MOP universe is harder work than trying to fix problems. MOP universe requires a lot of work to understand what the end point will look like – how your A, B and C of the game need to look in order to reach your dream. It then involves becoming very clear on how good you are right now completely objectively. No more living in bullsh*t world, thinking or feeling you are doing OK when you are not. From now on, you will use objective data and testing to know how good you are.

Getting to work in the MOP universe involves becoming very deeply embedded in the here and now, day-by-day working on the agreed plan. It involves great discipline not to change plans just because you feel like things are or are not working. During a practice session, MOP universe requires that the athlete and coach pay no attention at all to what is not working, or Moments of Sh*t. This is quite a challenge for most coaches and athletes, and many will tell you it is impossible. The rewards of living in MOP universe, however, are monumental!

THE GOOSE BUMP MOMENT

I am often asked, 'What is the most important part of sport?' I always answer, 'The performance zone', or what I call the 'Goose Bump Moment'. The Goose Bump Moment (GBM) is a pure zone moment. Having control over how you feel immediately prior to performing is critical to achieving performance potential and consistency under pressure. If you do not have the ability to control what you feel during pressure moments then your mind can become your worst enemy, especially if you are performing badly. Further, if you cannot control what you feel prior to performance, you never gain control over the performance 'zone'. Your mind tells you that it is completely outside your control.

When I refer to what you 'feel', I mean far more than just emotion; I mean whole mind-body-spirit harmony. A GBM is when an athlete drops deeply into 'instinctive' performance mode. Afterwards they talk about not remembering the moment at all, and say that time went incredibly quickly. They also say that, in the heat of battle, they felt they had 'all the time in the world' and had amazing peripheral vision, being able to see wider than normal. When an athlete achieves a pure GBM, they talk about it as though it were a 'different them' performing, a super-human them who could do almost anything they chose. Their skills are sharper, their power greater and their overall ability to perform higher. They talk about being a 'pure them', and say it is very addictive to be in that zone and far more exciting than the actual outcome of their sport. They become incredibly motivated to master it because it is the golden road to realising their true potential, and they make this the most important thing on their list when discussing success. Their sport becomes merely a vehicle to access this special place.

This is one of the most exciting chapters for me to write about. It is certainly one I have waited to share with great anticipation. (I had to write 'I will be patient and thorough' at the beginning of this chapter to make sure I did not rush writing it from over-excitement!) The GBM is the most important component of my work with athletes.

When I am working with an athlete, we start with discussions about their Pathway 1 philosophy and Impossible Dream, then quickly move to focus on moments when they have previously performed at their very best. I am looking for moments when they were in the zone and their performance was pure and flowed instinctually, when there was nothing they could not do and they were in harmony with the universe. It is during these discussions that many athletes explain that, as they talk about these moments, they get goose bumps, hence the term 'Goose Bump Moment'. It is important to point out that they do not get the goose bumps when performing; these occur afterwards, when thinking about or talking about key moments when they achieved that pure instinctual harmony. So don't feel disappointed if you think you never get GBMs because the goose bumps don't occur during performance. Athletes also say that it would be amazing to control the performance zone or GBM when they train and perform, as they know they would perform to their potential, and do much better than they currently are.

It is at this point that I explain to an athlete that the GBM is one of our most important goals! Sure, some days they may not be able to achieve a 100 per cent pure GBM, but they also learn that they still have to perform, and it does not become a way out for the mind under pressure to say, 'Oh well, I did not have a 100 per cent pure GBM, so I could not perform.'

We then talk about how all the key components of what we will cover in our work contribute directly to the GBM. Everything we do links in (e.g. Pathway 1 philosophy of courage, non-outcome success rules, MOP universe, Habits of Greatness (HOGs)) and works in harmony together. It becomes a powerful foundation to mental fitness and strength. This results in the mind letting go and dropping into instinct mode, thereby achieving a GBM. Over time the purity of the GBM deepens as a person matures and achieves deeper self-acceptance, becoming more comfortable and experienced in their sport or whatever it is they are mastering (e.g. a musical instrument). On the other hand, however, if someone is not living fully from courage in life and holds to outcome success rules, or has other insecurities that prevent self-acceptance (e.g. feels ugly or unlikable or like a fake), then pure GBMs are impossible to achieve.

I give the diagram overleaf to all athletes and other people I work with in the very first session so they understand what it is we are trying to achieve. The centre of the triangle becomes the only mind 'goal' we set and monitor over time. If they come in with performance anxiety or low self-confidence, I provide a caring and empathic ear for the first five minutes, then respectfully put that to the side and say we will get back to that later. I am determined to give minimal attention to what I do not want to see (e.g. fear of failing) and maximal attention to what I do want to see (e.g. the courage to go for it).

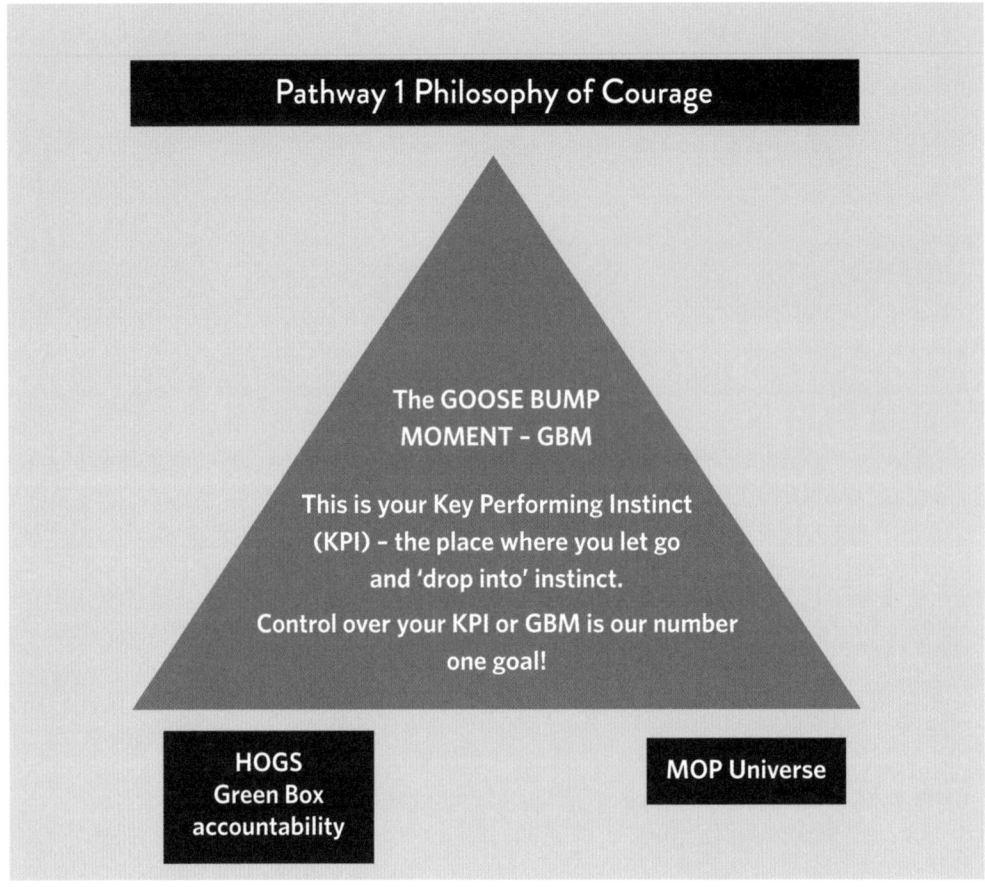

We then set a 'purity outcome measure' to reinforce that the GBM is all I am interested in. For example, in golf, players start to record the purity of GBMs achieved on their course map books, or what they refer to as their 'yardage books'. On the first tee shot on their first hole they might record 1 = 8 to show that their GBM was 8 out of 10 pure. Then they do the same thing for their second shot and for every shot on the round. After the round they generate a hole-by-hole average and an overall round purity rating.

In addition to recording GBM purity out of 10 as a performance stat, athletes also align their language and thinking to the idea that the GBM is the most important thing – more important than outcome. They agree that 70–90 per cent of their time talking and thinking needs to be about the GBM and learning (e.g. non-outcome performance lessons, character lessons about courage under pressure, etc). Reflecting on what they learn about getting into the GBM is absolutely critical to uncovering their true potential. We discuss times when their pre-performance routine has worked really well in training and practice, and make it a primary goal during actual events. We align performance language, discussed in the MOP universe chapter, to the GBM as well. The following examples show how someone might use their performance language when asked by a support person or coach how their day had gone.

'My best memory of my GBM today was . . .'

'What I learnt today was that when I did _____ it really helped me achieve greater control over my GBM and actually sped up how quickly I achieved a deep zone as the referee's whistle went off.'

'What I am most proud about is how hard I am working on mastering my GBM in practice, and how it is quickly becoming more important to me than the actual score or result!'

These examples show how you should think and talk when reviewing training, practice or actual performance. This is where using your performance language really begins to pay back. When you start to focus it in one key area, such as the GBM and learning, it becomes worth its weight in gold. It also helps parents and coaches not to have to come up with magical comments as it puts the pressure back on the person they are supporting to talk about their sport or activity in this mentally strong and optimistic way when asked.

When we have the GBM as the primary mind performance stat and the thing that is most thought and talked about, exciting things start to happen. The GBM becomes more important than the actual result, and even than the person's sport or other pursuit itself. The 'thing' they do essentially becomes just a vehicle to give the person access to this special GBM place. It is at this point that they truly start to live in a non-outcome universe. They start to let go of the results as important, and cannot wait to perform again to feel the way they do during the GBM.

Here is a brief passage from promising young New Zealand golf professional, Caroline Bon. After only one Skype call, Caroline took the material we discussed and ran with it. No, not ran – she sprinted with it! My greatest memory of working with her was the way she switched from thinking so much about outcome to not caring within such a short time. She virtually fell in love with the way she felt when she went to her GBM, or what she refers to as 'Purple'. It was her desire to feel this way again and again, and at big tournaments that fuelled her passion to train and play, and made working with her such a buzz.

THE POT OF GOLD AT THE END OF THE GBM RAINBOW!

Working with David has helped me discover and enjoy my ideal playing state – my simple term for it being 'purple'. Purple is playing care-free golf, not careless but care free, seriously not caring about the outcome and just going for it! Practising no longer feels like a chore; it's now an addiction to hunt the deeper purple place to be in and find how long I can be in that state. It is as though my mind now enjoys feeling that way more than it actually enjoys hitting the ball. Golf has merely become a vehicle to feel this way! I have also seen glimpses of my true playing potential when feeling this way, and that really excites me.

Caroline Bon

If you are ever going to master your pursuit and unleash your true potential, it is critical that you spend the rest of your performance days getting better and better at dropping into the GBM in your pre-performance routine. It is a deep, calm, self-believing place where you can actually 'turn off' your conscious mind and stop thinking, allowing your unconscious mind to execute from pure instinct, and not under any pressure.

There are two types of sport: continuous, such as soccer (90 minutes), rugby (80 minutes) and BMX (35 seconds); and those with many discrete executions, such as golf, tennis and cricket. In all sports, however, the GBM is just as important and the process of accessing it is exactly the same. The length of the performance space is the only thing that differs. Even in the longest sports, there are usually short bursts where players need to execute. For example, soccer is made up of many short and long segments, during which a player engages with the ball then does not have the ball. In both short and long duration sports, the key is to be able to control 'tipping' off into instinctual performance (e.g. just after a penalty restart). In this zone, time no longer exists anyway, so it does not matter how long the event is; what matters is learning how to be instinctive, and controlling the GBM gives you that tool.

In sports such as cricket and golf, where there is an extended period in between shots, the key is to be able to drop in and out of the GBM, as it is impossible to stay in pure focus for four hours or five days (a test match in cricket). With golfers, I have them establish a pre-shot routine that begins within five to ten yards of the ball and stops immediately after they have put their club back in their bag after the shot.

When instinct flows, magic truly occurs. Many minutes (in continuous sport) or executions (e.g. shots in tennis or balls faced in cricket) can go by without the athlete recalling the passing of time, and afterwards they struggle to remember what actually happened. When an athlete talks about this occurring, it is a sign that they were truly instinctive. They will often get goose bumps when talking about the performance afterwards, and it will not because of the way they played, but because of the 'spiritual' way they felt when playing. This is the magic I look for and it's why I do my job! That is why I was most excited to write this part of the book. I really hope you gain mastery over this special place, and for parents and coaches to experience it with their athlete too.

The following section introduces what I consider to be the three most important elements to mastering and unleashing your GBM in the pre-performance moment. Although I discuss these in the context of sport, they can also be applied to music, school or business – in fact, any activity in life!

The three key elements are: (1) your Pathway 1 philosophy; (2) deep relaxation; and (3) imagery. They are all powerful enough to offer reliable and effective routines in order to access pure GBM in their own right, but when combined offer a very special experience for the athlete. It is through the melding together of these three processes that the greatest GBM purity is achieved, and reliable and consistent performance is obtained. It is as though mastering these three elements opens the door to the soul!

GBM AND PATHWAY 1

By this stage of the book, you should have spent a great deal of time reflecting on your Pathway 1 philosophy. You should have a phrase or word or picture that inspires you to live and perform from deep courage. It should make you feel that what you think about or say to yourself when connecting to your philosophy is the most important thing in the world to you. Your Pathway 1 philosophy should be a portal through which you access deep, powerful, emotional calm and even spiritual centeredness, where your mind is at ease and your soul is calm and at peace.

I know that sounds pretty flowery, but when you access a pure Pathway 1 mindset, it feels pretty free! You can also understand from my description why the Pathway 1 philosophy is so critical to being able to access true instinct and a pure GBM. Without true deep courage, you will never establish an underlying sense of trust in yourself to just let go and act. If you get a chance, have a look at the following YouTube clip of base jumpers. There are two scenes in this clip that highlight the key moment of letting go with absolute trust in yourself and your equipment. Both scenes are in slow motion – in the first, a single jumper jumps off a cliff doing a back flip; and the second, three jump together doing a back flip. Each moment shows beautifully what I am talking about when I say 'letting go' and trusting. Watching this clip gives me goose bumps every time!

www.youtube.com/watch?v=h4WnFhiw_eY

It should be that living from your Pathway 1 philosophy is more meaningful to you as a person than anything else, even winning and earning millions of dollars as a professional athlete. I am not saying that winning and money are not important, because they are, just that they should never be more important than living a certain way. Living to your philosophy will lead you to feel far deeper pride and self-acceptance than winning a game, achieving a top-10 world ranking or earning millions of dollars will ever do. During your pre-performance routine, your Pathway 1 philosophy is your direct link to courage and the first powerful way to access and control the GBM.

Introducing Your Pathway 1 Philosophy into the Pre-performance Routine

Introducing your Pathway 1 philosophy into your routine in the period immediately before you perform is a critical step for obtaining performance consistency as it allows you reliable access to your performance zone, or GBM, when you perform. Depending on the sport you participate in, or the activity you are mastering, the way you introduce pure Pathway 1 prior to executing will more than likely differ based on the core feeling or spirit you are trying to achieve. For example, if you play rugby in the forwards, you will likely want to experience GBMs when you are combative and aim to physically dominate your opposition. As you approach the start of the game, you would need to inject your philosophy into physical drills and activities that unleash an aggressive, powerful creature.

For a lawn bowler, it may be that you want to unleash a very calm and spiritual monk-type creature that has great suppleness and fluid movements. Your Pathway 1 philosophy would need to be introduced through various drills and activities that allow the peaceful GBM to be achieved.

For a BMX rider about to race a super-X track, or a horse eventer about to do a cross-country course, they would need to access a deep courage to overcome a very real fear of being hurt or killed. Most riders experience this fear at some point (especially after a crash or fall) and so it is important for them to have a Pathway 1 routine to engage their courage and not allow fear to dominate their mind space, especially immediately before setting off. Once underway, these athletes say fear drops away as instinct takes over.

Doing the next activity, where you reflect on your deepest or most pure GBMs, will help you get clear on whether your Pathway 1 philosophy is enough to generate the feeling you need to perform, or if you need to add actions too.

THE GOOSE BUMP MOMENT: EXERCISE 1

Reconnecting with Your Pathway 1 Philosophy and Introducing It Into Your Pre-performance Routine

Write your Pathway 1 philosophy here:

Now write your 10 best MOPs when performing. That is, the 10 best examples of when you were in the zone, and everything just flowed. These will be times when you felt deep focus and pure instinct when you performed, and likely had a mindset disconnected from outcome.

1. _____
2. _____
3. _____
4. _____
5. _____
6. _____
7. _____
8. _____
9. _____
10. _____

Getting Your Pathway 1 Recipe Clear

Now spend some time thinking about the steps you went through before performing at the times you listed above. What did you do immediately prior to the start of the game or event that resulted in these MOPs? Write a short, step-by-step list of how you accessed the deep space. For example, did you:

1. breathe deeply
2. quietly say your Pathway 1 phrase to yourself
3. imagine seeing yourself execute perfectly
4. hear your parents or coach remind you that living and performing from your Pathway 1 philosophy is far more important than the outcome? (That is, did you link in with your non-outcome success rule?)

You are doing this to generate a step-by-step process for how you will access your Pathway 1 courage immediately prior to, or even during, performances from here on in. If you have already started to do this for your pre-performance routine then that is excellent, and you are ahead of where I wanted you to be by now. So, well done.

Here is an example from lawn bowls:

1. Stand quietly away from your competition as they do their bowl. To yourself, you say inside your mind, 'Be the lion' (your Pathway 1 philosophy).
2. Roll over in your mind what you see as most important here, right now in this next bowl. You remind yourself that success has nothing to do with the result, as that is merely an outcome. You tell yourself quite strongly, as that is how you have found this works best, that SUCCESS EQUALS INTENT!
3. Say to yourself, 'I actually don't care where this bowl ends up! And I don't care what people think about me or my bowl. What I care most about is that I give it every ounce of focus that I have and drill it.'
4. While doing the steps above and waiting your turn, polish your bowl with your cloth. You are mindfully aware of the smooth surface of the bowl, and it reinforces the things you are saying to yourself in your mind.
5. When it is your turn, walk to the mat in a very relaxed manner. Then just before you drop into your bowl say, 'Be the lion,' and send the bowl on its way!

Now it is your turn. Write your steps for accessing your Pathway 1 courage immediately prior to executing. (I have put seven numbers; feel free to use more or less.)

1. _____
2. _____
3. _____
4. _____

5. _____
6. _____
7. _____

This short, step-by-step Pathway 1 guide is now ready for you to start using and experimenting with in your pre-execution routine for your training, practice and actual performance. The key is to keep trying your Pathway 1 philosophy in different places in your preparation to see how it influences the actual pre-execution 'feeling' or 'zone'. Keep experimenting with different 'ingredients' until you have found the ones that work for you and have proven reliable under the highest pressure, not just for training or practice.

RELAXATION

After courage, relaxation is the most powerful feeling you need to master and control if you are ever going to reach your true potential. The impact deep relaxation has on the mind and body is massive. The impact that this then has on your performance is profound!

A deeply relaxed individual will be physically supple and mentally focused. Their unconscious and conscious mind, their body and their soul will all be aligned. These are all critical ingredients to learning during a coaching session and executing under pressure during performance. Relaxation is a powerful tool to introduce into your pre-performance routine in order to gain more control over that critical period immediately before you perform. You will achieve a physiological 'purity', with your muscles responding the same way each time you do what you do (e.g. the muscles in your fingers if you play a musical instrument). The more you master relaxing in this period, the greater consistency you will obtain due to your consistent mental state and deep peace of mind.

Many of the top athletes I work with have chosen to use simple

Relaxation in action: Hana Seifert reviews the yardage book in golf. She has found that using 'hooo hummm' relaxation (see The Goose Bump Moment: Exercise 2) at various times during the round, including before making shot decisions, has assisted her in making 'good' choices, especially under pressure.

relaxation as the foundation to their pre-performance routine. For example, in golf, many players relax as they take their club out of the bag, make their shot decisions, go through a supple and relaxed practice swing, address the ball and hit it. Working to maintain a relaxed mindset throughout allows them to hit from pure instinct without pollution or interference from thoughts. They hit the ball with full expression, free of any repression due to tension in the body or mind.

Learning to relax will help you perform better, no matter what you do. By itself however, relaxation is limited in the extent it can help you. What will allow you to maximise the powerful impact relaxation training can have is putting into practice the strategies and beliefs covered in the previous sections of this book. These provide a foundation for tapping into a level of deep relaxation that will surprise you. Most people believe that relaxation is simply a method to access a calm-feeling state. When you master relaxation from the foundation you have established through this book, however, you will find that it is actually a portal through which you can pass to access unlimited energy and 'eternal youth'! You will feel young, and you will be able to play your sport and be active for many more years than you previously thought possible. (You will see what I mean by eternal youth when you watch the YouTube clip in the highlighted section below.)

Having a Pathway 1 philosophy, living with the strong values of courage and patience, having a deep belief that success is based on your effort, not the outcome, and living in a universe dominated by MOPs, all establish the potential of infinite energy. Mastering the key elements to relaxation will give you the ability to relax deeply and achieve a 'still mind', thereby accessing this energy at times when you need it. For example, you might be on the verge of performing better than ever before when you suddenly have a powerful emotional reaction of excitement and hope that you will achieve a personal best, or you might be on the verge of defeat or victory in a very close championship final when the next mistake by one of the teams could cost them massively.

STILL MIND

www.youtube.com/watch?v=Mm3CmNE72Bw

This YouTube clip is about Moriji Mochida, a 10th Dan Kendo martial artist who at 89 years old was still practising the art! He talks about mastering deep relaxation and breathing to achieve a 'still mind', which allowed him to unleash infinite physical potential and practise his martial art against young men until a very old age. It is an inspirational clip.

Moriji Mochida did not start his journey to achieving a still mind until he was over 50 years old, after realising he had to as

> his body began to age and his physical strength started to leave him. Imagine if he had started his 'mind journey' when he was 20 years old! Don't you wait until old age erodes your vitality to begin mastering your own mind.

Anybody, no matter what their passion or pursuit, can have the same control over their mind and emotions that Moriji Mochida did. Imagine what you could achieve if you applied your mind to your life and passion with the same commitment and purity as he did. Many athletes ask me what they need to do to perform better under pressure. When I say to them that they need to learn how to relax deeply, they always nod and smile. They get it! It makes so much sense to them. Even if they are a social, weekend athlete, they get it.

Despite this awareness, however, very few athletes and people in general actually commit to learning how to relax deeply, let alone progressing their ability so far that they can do so under pressure. Very few understand just how much 'hard' work and discipline it takes to master deep relaxation. They often say to me that they 'just don't have time'. Surprisingly, this lack of effort to learn and master how to relax is equally prevalent in elite athletes as it is in social, weekend ones.

Further, many athletes believe that all they have to do when they are nervous is take a few deep breaths and that this will relax them. It will help, but it will not be enough. If you have not rewired your mind to put effort as the most important thing and outcome as the least important, then under pressure it will go to its default setting of outcome thinking. Usually, if winning, the outcome thinking is about not blowing it, and if losing, it is a fear of judgement. Hence, the primary default setting in most people is 'fear', often perceived by athletes as performance anxiety.

The mind will go to a deeply relaxed state only when it has firstly ingrained the idea that success equals non-outcome, and secondly intentionally mastered relaxation under adversity and pressure in practice and performance. Only then will it become the primary default setting. It takes considerable effort and practice over a long period to achieve this. Unless you commit time to mastering how to relax, it is not going to work for you under pressure when you need it.

Learning to relax is like any other skill: if you want it to become a deep, effective automatic habit or default, you must master it first under optimal conditions (i.e. in a quiet room at home). You can then gradually progress it through different levels of adversity/distraction to really embed it (e.g. in a loud public space in town, then your training and practice, followed by your actual performance moments).

THE GOOSE BUMP MOMENT: EXERCISE 2

How to Do Basic Relaxation

When I first did relaxation training with rugby players, I failed miserably! They laughed at me and told me to find something far more masculine, so away I went. This exercise outlines what I went back to them with. It works for large, front-row forwards in rugby; it works for lawn bowlers and golfers; it works for musicians; and, most importantly perhaps, it works for coaches and parents. The technique involves three very basic phrases. Some athletes use all; many choose the one that fits their mind best.

Hooo hummm

One, two

Sitting still, thinking nothing

Step 1: Learn to breathe properly

Simple relaxation involves being able to breathe correctly. Correct breathing involves an in-breath of three or four seconds through your nose until you feel your tummy button 'coming out' as the air fills your lungs completely and the diaphragm expands down into the stomach cavity. This results in the sensation of the tummy rising when breathing. Ideally you should hold your breath for two or three seconds and then breathe out slowly through a slightly closed mouth. Try to breathe out for longer than breathing in. The idea is that this is a gentle, smooth process. You should not almost pass out from breathing too long in or out, or holding your breath too long.

Step 2: Add a thought feeling-deepener to your breathing
To deepen your breathing and relaxation, you can introduce key thoughts. For example, on the in-breath think (you can't say it and breathe) *hooo* and on the out-breath think *humm*. The hooo sounds like the laugh of Father Christmas (i.e. hooo, hoooo, hoooo). 'Ho hum' is an old phrase I remember my mother using when I was growing up; it means 'don't worry about the little stuff'.

You may also want to try thinking *one* on the in-breath and *two* on the out-breath, or saying one of the following phrases slowly in your mind while breathing: *standing still, thinking nothing* (if you are standing), *sitting still, thinking nothing* (if sitting) or *lying down, thinking nothing* (if lying down).

The key with this last one is not to try to not think anything, rather it is to say this phrase to yourself in your mind while quietly standing, sitting or lying down – whatever position you are in. Let all the other thoughts and images in your mind just come and go. Do not try to fight thoughts you do not want; it will only make them stronger. Merely accept that they are there and go back to saying your phrase.

Try different phrases and decide which one best fits your mind and results in the deepest relaxed feeling. It is OK to combine them as well. What works for one person does not necessarily work for another. Find what works for you.

Step 3: Write your relaxation routine here:

Step 4: Practise often until you have mastered the skill

Once you have your routine clear, start practising three or four times a day for one to five minutes, in a place where it is quiet and you are reasonably free from distractions or interruptions. You can even time your practice to coincide with your cup of tea or coffee. In between sips, or even when savouring the tea or coffee in your mouth, roll your phrase over in your mind.

Step 5: Practise in more and more stressful places and environments

Once you have mastered relaxing in a quiet place, start to build its durability by taking it to situations and environments where you know you will be under pressure, or feel annoyed or uneasy, (i.e. find ways to start to test your mental fitness or strength and your ability to relax when upset, agitated, frustrated or distracted.)

List five places or situations that wind you up and could become 'mind gyms' to strengthen your ability to relax. For example, on the school bus at the end of the day when you are hungry and tired; trying to talk with your partner at the end of a very hard day at work; in a busy shopping centre.

1. _____
2. _____
3. _____
4. _____
5. _____

Step 6: Start to introduce relaxation into your practice and low-pressure performance space

Start introducing your relaxation routine into your pre-training or pre-performance routine if you play a sport or musical instrument. You can also inject it anywhere else you think it could be beneficial (e.g. in tennis, at change of ends or in between points). In fact, try it anywhere you think it will help you to stay calm and relaxed (e.g. walking between the green and tee in golf or sitting in the car on the way to training).

The key is not to expect too much too early with your relaxation. Over time, as you get used to using it, it will start to pay back and you will notice many benefits, such as improved sleep (especially the night before big events), feeling more relaxed under pressure, greater consistency in your technique, a better mood during a performance (especially when things are not going well) and so on. It is also very likely that as you learn how to relax deeply when training, practising and performing, you will also start to enjoy what you do more!

I recommend to parents and coaches that they learn basic relaxation as well. They always laugh at me when I suggest it, but they soon learn just how beneficial it is. Usually, the very next session I meet with them and their child or athlete, they say how useful it has been. Many report that they do not react like they used to, which improves their relationship with their child or athlete. It gives them a tool to use in situations such as sitting in the car on the way home after their child has had a poor performance or training session, which would usually create a tense atmosphere.

IMAGERY

Imagery involves using the mind or body to 'paint' or 'feel' a picture. For example, playing out a 'mental video' of what you want to happen, or 're-seeing' what has just happened. Some athletes may have quite limited imagery quality, however (e.g. blurry, black-and-white and vague), and 'think' pictures more than see them, while others may have extremely vivid colour imagery. Some athletes may be more kinaesthetic and feel through their body how they have done or will do something. When an athlete 'feels' behaviour, it is not in their mind, rather in their muscles themselves. If there is any thinking connected with body feel, it may be the affirmation when the muscles get it correct (i.e. 'Yes, that was how it felt, just like that'). It is important not to worry about how you do your imagery. It does not matter if you do it through your mind or bodily feel.

The key is that you spend time mastering your type of imagining in order to be able to refine it, grow it, grow control over it and then work at combining the skill with your Pathway 1 philosophy and relaxation in your pre-performance routine. The greatest thing about imagery is that you can also use it during events to assist your performance and build confidence and self-belief. For example, soccer players can use imagery before taking a free kick to visualise what they are going to do; golfers can use imagery in their pre-shot routine to help narrow their focus on the very next shot; all athletes can use imagery after a MOP, replaying it in their mind to boost confidence and assist learning (i.e. looking at what they just did technically to achieve that outcome). Imagery is a very important and powerful mental skill!

Just like with relaxation, it is critical that you learn how to imagine first with no pressure, then grow stronger at it under pressure. For example, spend time at home imagining while reflecting on your performance or watching YouTube clips. You can also introduce imagination when practising and training. Don't put pressure on yourself to generate a perfect visual or feeling when you first include it in your routines and play. If you stick at the skill and develop it over time, you will really start to 'see' what you want to do before you execute in a deep, rich way. This in itself will take your performance to an entirely new level of consistency and reliability. It certainly seems to be a core skill that all the great athletes have mastered.

'BEFORE EVERY SHOT I GO TO THE MOVIES IN MY HEAD.'

JACK NICKLAUS (World's greatest golfer ever)

THE GOOSE BUMP MOMENT: EXERCISE 3

Imagery Mind Gym: Improve Your Ability to See or Imagine Yourself Performing

The more you practise imagining, the better and stronger it becomes. There are many ways that you can practise. Here is one that I like.

Building Imagery by Working Back from Perfect Examples

Start off looking at examples of what the optimal execution or performance looks like for you in your sport or other pursuit on YouTube. YouTube is a phenomenal tool. You must use it if you do not already. It holds amazing footage of almost any sport or activity you can think of! It is often very rich in detail. Most clips have great music that engages the mind fully. There is slow-motion footage, often with the ability to slow it down yourself so you can watch and re-watch key moments in detail to see 'just how they did that'! This is a perfect tool for imprinting MOP images and information into your mind.

The next step after finding the clips you like is to watch them, repeatedly! Lock this into your daily schedule. If you download a YouTube downloader, you will be able to load them onto your phone or iPad and take them with you to training and practice. You can then watch them at important moments, such as just before you start training to inject inspiration and really engage your imaginative mind.

The next step is to try to see or feel yourself in your mind doing what the people you are watching are doing. As you get better at this, simply turn off the clip and try to do it without the aid of the film.

You can also spend periods of your day-to-day practice and training working really hard to introduce imagining and feeling. For example, in squash you could hit the same drop or smash shot again and again until your body can hold the 'feel' of the shot. Get yourself to hear the sound of the ball on the wall, feel it hitting the racket and feel the racket in your hand, then take the ball away and see how much your mind can 'imagine' still doing the shot. Then walk off the court, sit in the changing room and see how fully you can take your mind there again. See if you can do it so fully that your body moves gently, almost as though it is playing the shots and cannot actually tell if you are playing or not!

Once you achieve this level of imagery, your mind is starting to become really mentally fit and strong. Imagery is a well-supported mental technique that does improve skill development and actual performance under pressure. Those who spend time mastering imagery are able to see high levels of detail and complete plays and patterns in their minds very quickly. The other thing that happens with deep imagery is that an athlete usually uncovers the next 'extension' to their game or the sport itself. It is in deep imagery, especially when also relaxed deeply, that the greatest creativity occurs, and from this comes often quite amazing intuition.

Build your imagery mind gym here:

_____
_____
_____
_____
_____
_____
_____

ANCHORING PATHWAY 1, RELAXATION AND IMAGERY INTO YOUR PRE-PERFORMANCE ROUTINE

Now that you have an understanding of each of the elements critical to accessing the GBM, experiment using your Pathway 1 philosophy, relaxation and imagery as a basic pre-performance routine until you find what combination works best for you. You will know when you have a good routine because you will start to feel as though you have complete control over your emotions and thinking, and you are deeply settled when accessing that mind space just before you perform, whether that be as you are walking out on stage, crossing the white chalk or putting on your helmet. The mind space should be calm, relaxed, patient, powerful, confident and believing (and, if need be, aggressive and ruthless) all at the same time. Your evolving mindset should give you a sense that your potential is about to 'explode', and that you will start performing at a level that previously had merely been in your wildest fantasy!

The following passage from Luke Toomey provides an excellent example of how to combine the three critical elements discussed in this section.

THE MONK

'The monk' is a term David introduced me to that emphasises a state of deep thought, focus, relaxation and contentment. I often ask myself the question, 'Luke, how deep can you take the monk?' when I feel myself becoming nervous, over-excited, fearful or any other emotion that comes with pressure during vital moments of my practice and play. In order to bring myself into this state, I try to concentrate on long, slow breaths and think to myself *standing still* as I inhale and *thinking nothing* as I exhale. I then visualise exactly how the next shot will be executed, or 'play a movie' if you will, including as much detail as I can possibly imagine. This helps to dial in my focus and diminish my sense of the surrounding environment. From here I 'feel' when I am ready to address the ball. I then move in and address the ball, thinking nothing and feeling deeply centred inside myself. The shot then takes care of itself. The 'letting go' of myself into this mind-spirit space felt quite freaky until I got used to it. Now it feels pure!

The ninja monk golfer.

Luke Toomey

THE GOOSE BUMP MOMENT: EXERCISE 4
Building Your Pre-performance Routine

You can now build your pre-performance routine by combining the three critical elements: Pathway 1, relaxation and imagery.

Here is a golf example to help you see what I am talking about. It does not matter if you play chess or are a professional dancer, there is also a 'pre-shot' period in those sports when you need to gather your emotions and thoughts, and 'drop into' a space where you are instinctive in order to access your true potential.

The following pre-performance routine is an example from a world-class elite young amateur player:

Step 1: Make course-management and shot-selection decisions; get my club out of the bag.

Step 2: Say Pathway 1 phrase to myself. Really allow myself to drop into the deep feelings this generates – feelings of courage and focus.

Step 3: Simply relax while standing behind the ball using 'hooo hummm'.

Step 4: See, think and feel what I want to do with the shot, what I intend to have happen. This feels like an unconscious 'knowing' rather than having any words. In unconscious knowing, I am not aware of any thinking, imagining or feeling where the ball needs to go or what is required. I just 'know'. [This is absolutely fine and represents a deeply advanced mind-body connection. It is usually reflected in many hundreds, and often thousands, of quality hit golf balls.]

Step 5: Hold the scene in my mind and 'feeling' in my body while relaxing for as long as needed.

Step 6: Address the ball and, when I feel ready, hit it.

Use this example to help build your own pre-performance routine. Write it down here:

Making Relaxation and Imagery a Part of the Daily Routine

You should include relaxation and imagery training into your daily schedule. You will see how this is done in the chapter 'The Honey Badger Mind Week' towards the end of the book. This mind training or mental 'conditioning' is as important as going to the gym and training physically. Include imagery mind gym sessions in your weekly schedule, marking out times when you will practise relaxation and imagery. Also include relaxation and imagery in your patience mind gym sessions. For example, when doing marbles, you could visualise the MOPs from the day, going over them slowly and making sure all the fine details and feelings are relived and encoded in your mind and body.

Testing Your Ability to Relax and Imagine When Stressed and/or Distracted

As you learn how to relax and imagine, embrace the challenge of testing these skills out under pressure and stress. The greatest shift when truly living from Pathway 1 courage is that pressure and stressful situations take on a whole new meaning and experience. Rather than running away from stress and pressure, when living from Pathway 1, you embrace them as opportunities to grow and evolve.

Developing relaxation skills and your ability to see or feel what you want to then execute with your actions are critical to fully embracing Pathway 1. Put the skills through the 'fire' as often as you can! You will not regret it as this will speed up their development and embed them deep in your unconscious mind. Once they become habit, you will notice that you feel naturally relaxed under pressure and you will start 'seeing' or 'feeling' what will happen next without having to consciously focus on it; it will just happen out of habit. Over time, it will start to feel as if it is not even happening, it will be so natural. It will be pure!

Putting your skills through the fire could involve relaxing on a busy bus or sitting in a busy shopping centre in town. In fact, it can be anywhere and doing anything that usually leaves you wound up and on edge.

Further, as you become more proficient at relaxation and visualisation you should start to find ways to try to distract yourself when practising and performing. For example, you could have the radio blaring loudly beside you or you could have someone come and start talking at you while you are trying to go through your pre-performance routine. The various ways you could test yourself and see how far your mental strength has come are endless.

In summary, the pre-performance routine is the most important way to unleash your mind fully, no matter what it is you do. Unfortunately, it also receives the least attention by most athletes and people in general, simply because they just don't know how to get their mind into that space, or how to train themselves to become mentally fitter and stay there when it is most needed. Most athletes spend time mastering how to do what they do (e.g. swinging a club or racket) and commit minimal time to mastering and training their minds, despite saying that the mind is the most critical variable for success. This is especially so in the modern era of sport where, world-over, most athletes are of equal size, speed and power. The mind has become the point of difference between success and failing, winning and losing!

Because most athletes ignore the mind, they have an inconsistent routine that varies depending on what just happened in the previous shot or moment, or on how important the game is that they are playing (e.g. a semi-final or first round-robin game). Many athletes also try different things in their pre-performance routine, minute by minute, day by day and event by event, and as a result never find mental or physical performance consistency.

Master the pre-performance mindset and you will master control over the GBM. Master the GBM and you will unleash your optimal potential and see just how good you are, and just how far you can go. It is critical that you commit the required amount of time, patience and reflection for building a pre-performance routine that fits you. A great pre-performance routine should be simple and brief and allow you to stop thinking during the time immediately before you execute. Consequently, you will engage pure Pathway 1 instinct and allow your body to do what you have spent so many hours training it to do, and get the mind out of the way!

TRAINING-TO-WIN AND THE IMPORTANCE OF DEEP PRACTICE

It was during a Super 15 rugby training session in 2012 that I had a sudden realisation about 'training-to-win'. I had often used the term in workshops and with athletes and coaches across many sports. I had also heard many athletes and coaches use the term. They would often define training-to-win as high intensity work and effort during practice or training, or high focus and killer instinct during performance. This makes sense to most people. What struck me though, on this particular day in 2012, was that most of these people had no idea what they were really talking about, especially me! We all thought we knew what we were talking about, but in reality we were just touching the surface of what training-to-win really means.

A short time after this realisation, I was at a presentation about what it takes to win a gold medal; included in the presentation was a video clip of New Zealand cyclist Sarah Ulmer winning her gold medal at the 2004 Athens Olympics. She annihilated her opponent! Sarah won gold and smashed the world record at the same time. Anyone who saw the race will most likely remember Sarah's physical condition when she finished. She could not breathe! Her gasping for air was audible as she made her way around the victory lap. Most people thought she was in shock that she had won. Her open mouth was her trying to breathe. She had raced so hard, and given so much that her body had not been able to 'keep up' with her spirit; she had raced on raw soul energy. It was while watching this clip that I finally understood what training-to-win really was.

When the lights came back on after this video, I was crying! I looked around and saw that I was the only one doing so. My tears were a direct response to the presence of 'riding-to-win', the presence of Sarah Ulmer's spiritual and emotional energy. This was the last part of the puzzle of what exactly training-to-win and performing-to-win were. I realised that it was perhaps one of the most critical components of any championship team or world-class individual athlete. If they cannot achieve a train-to-win mindset, they will never uncover their potential, and if they are up against world-class competition, they will never be a champion.

In its purest sense, training-to-win is an energy. It is not what you do, or even how you do what you do. It is the presence of something indescribable and intangible. It is something deeply 'spiritual'. When I use the word spiritual, I am not referring to anything religious, rather the presence of energy. When you see training-to-win and performing-to-win in actual performance contexts, you recognise this energy immediately; it has a massive impact on you. You 'feel' it in an unconscious and non-verbal place. Conversely, when it is not there you are struck by how different everything looks and feels in its absence.

When it is there, people do what they do, either as an individual or as a team, with no connection to outcome. They are acting unconsciously and disconnected from outcome altogether. If it is a team they become fused together, as if they are one creature with a single beating heart. It is at these times, when watching team sport, that I see something incredibly special unfold before my eyes and I get a chill down my spine. The team steps into a space where they start playing for each other; the 'brotherhood' or 'sisterhood' becomes the most important thing, and it is this connection across the group that makes special things happen. It is the basis for great comebacks and once-in-a-lifetime performances. Funnily enough, though, these performances seem to start happening quite frequently for teams and individuals that have mastered training-to-win. It is ironic that it is called training-to-win since, in its pure form, athletes are not doing what they do to win at all, or to try to avoid losing for that matter. I like the term, despite the irony, as it highlights that although winning is not the most important thing, and nor should it ever be, it is still important. The term also reinforces that achieving a large dream (e.g. to become the best in the world at something) requires a certain level of training and performing 'intent', otherwise it will never happen.

Training-to-win was certainly present for the Magic netball team in 2012. I could feel it when I walked into a training session. It was as though no one else outside the team existed. With every win on the way towards the Championship final, after losing their first four games straight, the training-to-win grew in intensity and presence. Conversely, it was not there in 2013 – I could not feel it when I walked into training, and it certainly was not there when they played. In 2013, it was as though they were trying to make things happen, to force it. We didn't even come close to finding what existed in 2012.

For the Chiefs Super Rugby team, they won both the 2012 and

2013 Championships. Training-to-win was strongly present both years.

> As a result of my 2012 rugby epiphany and Sarah Ulmer's 2004 gold medal race footage, my current definition of training-to-win and performing-to-win crystallised in my mind:
>
> **Training-to-win (and performing-to-win) is when the mind surpasses previously held physical 'limitations' and the body can no longer keep up . . . the body is then forced to extend into the 'unknown'. . . into the space between current reality and potential!**

The key to achieving this spiritual, emotional mind energy in competition is to master accessing it in training and practice first. Hence one of the last chapters in this book is about practice – more specifically, deep, deliberate and effective practice. All too often, the opposite is what most athletes do. Most athletes simply practice without thinking about it. For example, golfers swing their clubs at a range and just hit balls, often thousands of them each week. Bike riders just ride their bike around and around and around. Swimmers just swim and rugby players just pass and kick.

Very few athletes actually 'train'. Training involves learning, and learning involves a deliberate plan-action-reflection process. Most athletes don't grow significantly over time after peaking in their early twenties or late teens because they do not master training-to-win and end up hoping that simply doing what they do will help them improve. There is no action-learning involved. Sure, improvement still occurs, but it is most often 'chance' learning when a player 'stumbles' upon a learning. Because they usually have no awareness of how it occurred, improvement is incredibly slow and frustrating for everyone concerned (parents and coaches included).

Hope-based learning is most evident in athletes who live in the **red** (never does enough) and **yellow** (does just enough, or goes through the motions). People who are 'living' action-learning in practice and performance always live in the **green**! It is no surprise then that training-to-win is another term often used to describe the green 'always does extra' column of the chart included earlier in this book.

Deep practice occurs when deliberate, intense and focused attention is given to the process of what is occurring in order to facilitate a mental 'letting go', or release of mental control to the unconscious, instinctual mind. I believe that it is here, in the unconscious mind, where the spiritual energy I spoke of earlier resides. Hence it is very important to learn how to do deep, deliberate practice in order to master how to drop into a train-to-win and play-to-win mindset in competition, and whenever else you choose.

Technical thought is never involved at this level of deep instinctual practice and performance, and is in fact a block to training-to-win and playing-to-win. Technical thinking inhibits unconscious instinctual process. Technical practice is still important for skill development however (e.g. changing your swing or working on a small shift in your technique in tennis), so please make sure you realise I am not telling you not to do it. It is, however, quite different from train-to-win practice and needs to be treated differently. When someone is learning technical elements of their swing, you cannot expect a train-to-win mindset to be present. They may still be focused, and some athletes get incredibly focused, but because they will be locked in their conscious mind, trying to understand and figure things out, they will not drop into their unconscious, instinctual mind. This chapter does not cover technical training; it explains how to generate a train-to-win unconscious energy through deep practice, during which the athlete is actually not conscious of their surroundings – they are in the 'zone'. Often at this depth of training their mind cannot actually tell if they are training or performing for real. When an athlete tells you training is like that, they are training-to-win!

DEEP PRACTICE IN ACTION

I asked Brad Kendall to describe how Mark Brown looks when he practises. This is what he said: 'Serious!'

Yep, looks pretty serious to me too! Mark Brown at Kinloch as part of his British Open preparation in 2013.

THE KEY INGREDIENTS OF DEEP PRACTICE
The following are key ingredients necessary for achieving deep practice:

1. Deep practice requires clarity about what exactly you are trying to achieve.
Deep practice occurs when a person comes to training and practice with very clear targets, objectives and goals for what they will tick off that day. What they aim to achieve that day is directly linked through their weekly plan to their quarter-year plan, and their quarter-year plan links to their year plan. Everything that is done matters, and is relevant to the big picture.

It is when people have this clarity that they start to reap the rewards of their work. In order to achieve this level of clarity, though, you have to take the time to establish an extremely detailed and clear strategic plan, as discussed in previous chapters of this book. The greater an athlete's clarity about their long-term dream and end point as well as their current skills (i.e. test numbers, stats and pictures of the fundamental A, B, Cs) the more readily they will be able to drop into deep unconscious practice. The greater their clarity about what exactly they are trying to achieve each day, each hour, and every five minutes, the deeper their practice becomes and the deeper their engagement with their instinctual and unconscious learning capacity.

Training and practice become pure and free from distraction associated with lack of clarity and indecision. It is at this point that we can see and appreciate just how important a person's Pathway 1 philosophy is, and how critical attention to detail is when doing the hard yards discussed earlier in this book – from evolving the strategic plan to success, to mastering relaxation and visualisation. If you have been slack in the foundation setting, you will not achieve the degree of clarity required to start the process of dropping into train-to-win mode when practising.

DEEP PRACTICE: EXERCISE 1

Self-Reflection

Reflect on how thorough you have been putting into practice the strategies outlined in previous chapters of this book. Rate yourself on the scale below.

Poor (red)--------------Average (yellow) -------------Excellent (green)

If you have done a poor to average job, you will not achieve deep practice when you train. It is likely that you will experience good days and bad days, with brief periods of deep focus, but more often than not, you may feel as though your training and practice involve just going through the motions. If this describes you, then it is also likely that you spend a lot of time focusing on Moments of Sh*t, and probably often feel frustrated at your inability to 'get it' and 'fix' repeated errors.

If this is you, you need to go back and focus on the previous chapters of this book again! Your effort on the exercises in this book so far will tell you a lot about yourself and your habits, and what has helped or hindered your life and career to date (whether that be in sport, music or whatever else you are pursuing).

Note any excuses you have made to allow yourself to do a poor or average job on the exercises so far, as these will be the same excuses you use in other areas of your life, such as a poor or average income or relationship. There will be patterns and they are all linked. It is time to break the cycle of just going through the motions because you are undermining your own potential.

If you have done an excellent and thorough job on the exercises so far, however, it is likely you will achieve really deep practice when we start working through the various steps involved. It is also likely that you are probably already doing some or all of the steps covered.

Write here some general comments and reflections to yourself regarding your effort and thoroughness so far:

---

2. Deep practice requires strong discipline.

Deep practice occurs when a player is disciplined enough to be able to create a work space that is completely in line with what they want to do (e.g. not next to a friend with whom they chat and joke). Athletes who achieve deep practice stand out from other 'normal' athletes for a number of reasons. The first reason is that they do not tolerate interruptions or distractions during their work. They see time and practice as the most important resources they have under their control. They know that time is limited and ticking, and they hate time being wasted because they will never get it back. These athletes establish a practice space that clearly communicates 'DO NOT DISTURB ME!' If for some reason people do not get the message, they are often asked politely to talk to them when they have finished.

How disciplined are you at creating a practice space that allows you to deeply focus on the job at hand? Do you plan your practice based on being with friends or on what you need to achieve from your weekly, monthly and quarterly plan?

DEEP PRACTICE: EXERCISE 2

Building Your Own Powerful Practice Plan and Environment

What would the perfect practice plan and environment look like to support you to access deep practice when working? For example, would you go really early to the track when no one was there? Would you do your gym session during day when the range is busiest, so there is less distraction straight away? Would you avoid going with friends?

Write your practice plan below.

World-Class Practice Plan

1. _____
2. _____
3. _____
4. _____
5. _____
6. _____
7. _____
8. _____

Now start following this plan!

3. Deep practice looks like it is from another planet.

In addition to high clarity and an environment designed to increase work output, there are other characteristics that make someone in deep practice look as though they are from another planet.

An athlete operating from deep practice ironically executes far fewer repetitions than an athlete not training-to-win (e.g. a golfer who just stands there and hits ball after ball with no or little thought). When in deep practice, you will still 'do enough', but this will likely involve fewer reps than before. The way I am encouraging you to practice will take discipline because your default urge or unconscious mind will try to get you to do more, not less, in order to still feel as though you are doing all you can to get better. Deep practice holds true to that familiar saying: 'Less is actually more'.

When you nail a MOP and are operating from deep practice, you should actually stop and refrain from doing another execution immediately. It is critical to emphasise here that a MOP does not have to be a perfect outcome. It can be the smallest shift in the right direction. For example, you may find that your set-up or take-away was perfect, but the rest of the execution was substandard. In MOP universe, we focus in on that little shift and ignore the later MOS.

You then redo that MOP while reviewing it in your mind and body as fully as you can. Reconnect exactly with the feeling underneath the execution. Focus on analysing what you actually did that worked to gain mechanical understanding and an imprint on your brain about what you did and how it felt. Lock this into your memory by repeating these little phrases to yourself when you reach a clear understanding of what just happened in your MOP:

> 'That's it! Right there!'

> 'That is how that happened!'

> 'This is how it will be!'

This whole process may take 10 to 30 seconds. This is a really long time. You may even choose to step away from the 'hit zone' and relax deeply while trying to visualise what you just did. I want you to engage your entire body sensors in this reflection and post-MOP review. The way it sounded, looked and felt – every detail needs to be digested and savoured in your mind, body and soul. Move your body in any way you can to reconnect with the moment and what you are working on. Once you have completed this post-MOP process, step back into the hit zone and go back through your routine with your main focus now on trying to replicate the previous MOP routine, especially the way you felt.

4. Deep practice focuses solely on MOPs.
This point could also be part of the previous point, as it is another reason why deep practice looks like it is from another planet. Deep practice is achieved only when you are in MOP universe, and controlling what you focus on during your practice. Most athletes focus on Moments of Sh*t. After executing badly, they get angry and redo what they just did, usually with increased force and velocity! They get more tense with each MOS, and more desperate to fix what they just did wrong in order to try to have a 'good' practice or training. To make sure they get the message, they may even shout at themselves in their mind – or out loud if they have made the same mistake five times in the past 10 minutes. You know how it goes! There is no way that an athlete training and practicing like this will ever achieve deep practice, and no way they will ever reach a train-to-win level, let alone a play-to-win level in an actual performance.

In deep practice, you focus only on the MOPs. A lot of coaches and athletes laugh at this statement, and say, 'If I focus only on MOPs, how can I learn?' It is in this question that I see their deep belief that they only learn through mistakes. When I ask them, 'Why can't you learn through success or when things go right?' they say, 'Of course you can. Yes, you can learn through success.' Often, though, I can tell from the look on their faces and what they then talk about – usually how if they ignored mistakes like I suggested then the problem would not go away – tells me that they really struggle with the idea that learning through success is possible.

Clearly, coaches and athletes who struggle with the idea of not focusing on mistakes believe that they have to learn through error and that they will learn the most by doing so. Deep down they are scared that unless they 'fix' any problems they will never get better. And there it is – this is the main reason why people get so stuck on looking at Moments of Sh*t. As a result they end up locked in a 'fix-it' mindset. A fix-it mindset is the complete opposite of a growth mindset, in which someone aims to grow skills and evolve their game through focusing on what is working and taking them in the right direction, even if at a given moment they are only getting it right two out of every ten attempts!

DEEP PRACTICE: EXERCISE 3

What Are Your Beliefs About How People Learn Best?

When I suggest not focusing on errors at all and ignoring them completely, what does your mind reply to me? Does it say, 'This guy is dreaming; he is on another planet'? Does it tell you to stop reading because I don't know what I'm talking about?

Or does your mind warm to the idea of learning through Moments of Perfection and ignoring Moments of Sh*t? Does it feel as though a weight has just lifted off your shoulders? Do you start to see that you do have a choice and you can learn by focusing on what is working when you hit a MOP?

For deep practice to work for you as I want it to, you have to believe that you can learn and grow through MOPs.

Write a few comments to yourself here about whether you believe you have to look at errors to learn, or if you can actually grow by ignoring them completely and focusing on MOPs. Also write down whether you are willing to give it a try.

---

5. Deep practice means that you ignore every MOS.
The fifth core element of deep practice is to ignore Moments of Sh*t completely! If you execute a MOS, as quickly as possible go back to your pre-performance routine, refocusing on your last MOP and re-engaging with that memory rather than getting stuck on the MOS. The idea is to pay no attention to the MOS whatsoever, so the mind does not encode anything from it into the longer-term memory.

Consequently, that MOS will be forgotten and, at the end of training, it will hard for you to remember it. Over time, you will flood your memory with so many MOPs that your self-belief and confidence will be very high! That is exactly what you need to reach new levels. Athletes who focus heavily on each MOS fill their memories with them, and not surprisingly end up with self-doubt and fear-of-failure because their minds are saturated with evidence that they cannot perform well or improve. Further, if you live in MOS universe, you will more than likely notice that it is difficult to actually get yourself to do what you know deep down you must do to improve. It will feel as though you are losing interest in your pursuit, and you will sometimes find it hard even to go and see your coach or go to training. Deep down, the MOS focus will have started to wear you down.

> ## INTERESTING MIND FACT
>
> The mind has two main types of memory: the working memory and the long-term memory.
>
> Information is first held and processed in the working memory. This, however, has a limited capacity. If information is not focused on while in the working memory, it is discarded as new information comes in. The mind cannot keep holding on to information that receives no attention. It is seen as unimportant and deleted.
>
> It is this process that makes MOP universe so powerful. If we only pay attention to MOPs in the working memory, then any MOS will be deleted and not transferred to the long-term memory. Done well, this means that it will be very difficult, if not impossible, to remember your bad shots after a round (if playing golf for example). And as time goes by, it will become impossible to recall a MOS from previous performances. The same is also true about MOPs you do focus on. You will get to the end of your performance and be able to only recall MOPs. They will be vivid and powerful and, because they will have been transferred to your long-term memory, you will be able to recall them in many months' time. Eventually you will have a 'hard drive' full of MOPs!

6. Deep practice requires that you master relaxation.
You can enhance the depth of your learning when you reflect on a MOP immediately after executing it while relaxing at the same time. I touched on relaxation earlier and will comment further on it here. I ask that all athletes I work with master relaxation. I want them to be able to relax deeply within one or two breaths. It is critical that they are able to do this so they can drop deeply into their unconscious mind when performing and execute from deep instinct. I also want them to master relaxation to support MOP universe deep practice, which maximises learning and encoding.

Relaxation will open your unconscious mind, as occurs during self-hypnosis, and speed up the transfer of learning and encoding of information. While deeply relaxed, it will be as though you are 'pouring' information into your mind (i.e. correct technique) and body (i.e. correct muscle feel and tension, and transfer of power). Together, these things speed up skill development massively.

7. Deep practice is about practising your art, not just learning how to do the mechanics of it.
Most athletes practise 'doing' not 'performing'. For example, many golfers stand on the range for hours and hours swinging the golf club. This type of golfer is just mastering how to swing the club! This is perhaps the greatest fundamental mistake in golf. Many golfers practise for hour upon hour and hit thousands of golf balls standing on a flat mat, under cover and out of the conditions at a golf range – a completely different context and environment from that in which they actually play. Then, when they get to the golf course, they wonder why they are unable to match their range consistency and quality. This is because they have not practised playing. They have practised swinging the golf club. Golf is no different from any other sport or pursuit. To truly master it, you must first master training performance.

It is critical that you practise in different conditions and as many different contexts as possible. For example, in golf, on uphill, downhill and side-hill lies; in tennis, on different surfaces; in music, in different music halls and out busking on different streets with different audiences. Make sure you practise in all types of weather and against many kinds of adversity (e.g. hunger, tiredness and thirst). Make sure your practice includes sessions where you put pressure on yourself to 'have to make the next one' (e.g. you have one chance to nail the piano piece you are mastering for a concert). This does not mean that you should not also practise under optimal conditions (e.g. at home or on the range). You need to spend some time in optimal conditions as part of developing 'good enough' technical ability, but it should be as part of a holistic weekly practice programme.

8. Deep practice is about fully linking practice and performance.

Deep practice is about linking training with performance. It is about teaching your mind that performance is an extension of training and practice. In order to do this, deep practice must merge into events. This is achieved by following the same deep practice process when you play. It is easy to do. After a MOP, take your time to enjoy the moment and absorb as much information from the MOP outcome as possible (e.g. the way it felt, sounded and looked, focusing on the GBM). For example, in golf, after a MOP tee shot, stay on the tee watching the ball until it has stopped moving. If the next player comes onto the tee I tell players I work with to stand their ground and not get pushed around. Make them wait until you have finished watching and absorbing your MOP.

Further, what makes this even more important is that most athletes usually spend more time watching and focusing on a MOS. They will re-swing many times after a MOS, trying to 'learn their lesson' so as not to make the same mistake again. It is important that you give no time or attention to a MOS – move on as quickly as possible, either focusing on something else completely different (e.g. in golf, talking to your caddie about a movie, or in soccer running into position for your next job). I often laugh with golfers when talking about how to deal with MOS moments. I encourage them to pick up their tee as quickly as possible and walk back to their bag. I suggest watching the ball only long enough to get some idea about where it went, or even not watching it at all if playing with other golfers. What I have found is that most people you play with are more than happy to show you where your bad shots have gone. It is as though they take pleasure in your tragedy on the course!

In summary, in deep practice, when a MOP occurs (and this can be the smallest shift in the correct direction with something technical as well as actual outcome) the athlete stops and tries incredibly hard to understand how what just happened happened. They digest it bit-by-bit in their mind and body while relaxing as deeply as possible in an attempt to almost hypnotise themselves. This in turn floods the mind and brain sensors with all the rich information about what worked.

In the excitement of it all, the long-term memory devours the memory fully, resulting over time in the mind being full of MOP 'evidence' that the athlete can reach their dream. An athlete living in the MOP universe 'loves' the game, and is full of ambition with enormous internal motivation and enthusiasm to practise. As a result of this, they do more deliberate, quality practice, which in turn results in more and more MOPs, thereby creating and maintaining a prophecy or cycle of growth and potential. Perhaps what is most exciting is that deep practice facilitates training-to-win and this then underpins playing-to-win.

There are critical elements to achieving deep practice. For example, having a thorough long-term success plan and having everything linked so that you know what it is you are trying to achieve in the here and now. Another critical element for deep practice is in the way you practise: you should look like you come from a different planet. It is the differences between deep practice and 'normal' practice that make deep practice so incredibly hard to achieve. Most people want to take the easy road of looking like everyone else and working only to fix their mistakes from the previous week in order to perform better the next week. The hard road is living by the ideas covered in this chapter and book; it is committing to being different in a great way and giving yourself every chance to uncover your potential. Whether you have chosen the hard road or the easy road will be evident within one minute of watching you practise!

THE HONEY BADGER MIND WEEK

The saying 'Saving the best for last' has never more true than now. I believe this last chapter is going to be potentially the most important and life changing for you. It is one of my more recent developments in my work with elite athletes and people choosing to be 'great', and has come from them asking for ways to train their minds to become more mentally strong. Often our sessions would have covered much of what is in this book. They would have established their Pathway 1 philosophy and be living in their green box, but many would have behaviours they wanted to do that were not everyday behaviours. They were still critical for their long-term success – success-makers if you will – and more like Habits of Greatness (HOGs). I'm not sure yet how many MOPs are needed to make a HOG!

It was from these discussions that the idea of generating a mind week evolved. Some behaviours on the mind week would be daily, some two or three times a week, and some only once a week. All were vital!

HONEY BADGER MIND WEEK

Most Important List

1. Pathway 1 honey badger sessions (intentionally training 'letting go' into instinct and your KPI or GBM)
2. Intentional failing sessions (learning not to care about failing. Remember you can't tell anyone, 'I don't care')
3. X factor and love of game (injecting passion)
4. Patience mind gym (training focus and learning patience – 'I will be patient/thorough')
5. Relaxation and imagery (MOPs – relaxing or doing patience drill, image GBM, daydream with purpose)
6. ? = optional to include – up to what works for you on game- and recovery-day

MON	TUES	WED	THURS	FRI	SAT	SUN
5	5	5	5	5	6	6
2	1			2	4	
		1	3		3	
	3				2	
		2			1	
			1		KPI Imagining	
1						
		3			GAME	
4	4	4	4	4	6	6

THE HONEY BADGER

Before we look at each component of the mind week, it is important to introduce the honey badger. Where does the honey badger metaphor come from? The URL below takes you to a short YouTube clip about the honey badger – an animal I did not know existed until a rugby coach talked to me about it in 2013. Since then I have shown many teams and athletes this clip when talking about mental strength or toughness. Every athlete or team I have shown it to has loved it. They all connect with the tenacious spirit of the honey badger, who, no matter what the odds, always lives from courage. It is a true Pathway 1 creature, always on the 'front foot'. Its favourite food is the incredibly venomous cobra snake. Rather than ruin the video for you, I shall let you watch it. Essentially, it has come to represent the level of mental 'grit' athletes and other people I work with choose to pursue and want to achieve. They all smile when they see it for the first time, and often say the same thing: 'I want to be like that!'

While watching the clip, see if you can imagine how the honey badger would behave in your sport, or whatever it is you are pursuing. Even if your pursuit is a non-physical one (e.g. playing the flute), you can still make links to how it embraces challenges and deals with error or failing (such as when you are learning a difficult or new piece of music). Enjoy.

Introducing the Honey Badger
www.youtube.com/watch?v=VzEqmpnnYWI

THE HONEY BADGER MIND WEEK

As mentioned above, the Honey Badger Mind Week originated from discussions with athletes wanting physical ways to train their minds. Many had read books and talked to various people about the importance of the mind, but most had been unable to generate daily ways of training it to support its development and performance. When you look at the diagram of the mind week, you can see how it is designed to assist both. It provides a structure for daily mind exercises to grow mental fitness over time, and then a way to use this 'training' over the week to facilitate mental readiness for each performance. In this particular hypothetical week, the athlete is training throughout the week for a Saturday mid-afternoon performance.

The next section will briefly go through each element of the mind week.

1. Pathway 1 Honey Badger Sessions

People are funny creatures. Most people are habitual procrastinators. We often put off doing what will help us achieve our dreams. What is worse, though, is that we also often do what we know is not helping us achieve our potential. In fact, people often do things that are damaging to dreams, even to the point of sabotaging ourselves. People also often say that they are 'powerless' and unable to prevent these 'bad habits' from occurring (e.g. sleeping in; not following through on an eating plan, and even eating badly; procrastinating with key projects; not doing enough practice, etc). The list of ways these bad habits occur is pretty long! Usually people say the same thing: 'I am capable of so much more than I am achieving at the moment, but I just cannot find the way to achieve or reach it.'

The underlying issue with people not being able to change bad habits is related to unconscious levels of comfort and discomfort. It is as though they have an unconscious ceiling for what they see as their limit. Above that level, they become uncomfortable, and behave in ways to get themselves back to their comfort zone. The word 'uncomfortable' is appropriate, as at times the discomfort with moving above the ceiling, or comfort zone, is literally painful. They can also move below their comfort zone and experience similar feelings of discomfort. It is as though humans have a 'band of operating' that fits their unconscious expectations for themselves, or where they believe at a deep level they need to be to 'fit in' and be accepted by those around them. It is very much like a thermostat.

The unconscious mind establishes the 'thermostat setting' for the level at which someone operates as they grow up. Early experiences through childhood and then adolescence all contribute to 'setting' the unconscious thermostat level that influences later life behaviour in a major way. For example, research shows that most men only ever end up earning a little more money than their dads, so as not to embarrass them! Humans set comfort levels for everything: their wealth, the types of courses they enrol in at university, the type of partner they want to be with, etc. The ceilings they have are not real, however; they are glass ceilings. They are merely creations of the mind, and the mind builds up evidence that they exist over many years. Here is an example from my own life of what I am talking about.

SWIMMING ALONG, THINKING NOTHING!

As a child, I remember going to swimming lessons and hating them! I remember it being a literally painful and often embarrassing experience for me. I was a terrible swimmer. Over the years, I decided that my lack of skill in the pool was related to me having 'heavy muscle density'. I convinced myself that that was why I sank faster than I moved forward along the pool. I have no idea where I got this muscle density idea from!

When completing my psychology training in Auckland, I would swim most days for general fitness in an old 50-metre pool in Newmarket. There was a black line on the bottom of the pool marking the shift from the shallow end to the deep end. I would get to this line and have to stop and rest before swimming across the deep end. Inside my mind, I was panicking. I would think that I would drown! Then I would swim back to the line and rest again before completing the length. My best I could do was between six and ten lengths. I could never get over ten, and it would take me a good half an hour in the pool to achieve that.

As part of our final stage of training as a clinical psychologist,

> we were encouraged to take therapy. So once a fortnight I headed out to West Auckland to see a psychologist for my own counselling. One day, he said to me, 'David, Buddha had this saying: "Sitting still, thinking nothing". I think you would find it useful.'
>
> I paid my money and went back to Newmarket for my swim. On the way there, I thought that I would try this little phrase, but instead of 'Sitting still, thinking nothing', I would use 'Lying down, thinking nothing' and 'Swimming along, thinking nothing'. I got into the water and started swimming.
>
> Two and a half hours and 50 lengths later, I got out of the pool. I hadn't stopped once!
>
> The day before I had swum only six lengths, in halves. I was dumbfounded. I stood there, unbelieving of what had just happened. It was a key moment in my life. It was then I asked myself, 'Hell, if I have had this self-imposed limitation or ceiling on my swimming and what I am physically capable of, in what other areas am I living way under what I could actually achieve?'

The Pathway 1 sessions, also known as 'red sessions' or 'honey badger sessions', are designed to smash through these glass ceilings and give the mind a 'real experience', often an uncomfortable and painful one of going beyond previously held limits. They are named red sessions after the red line on the rev counter in a car. During these sessions you take yourself to the 'red line' or limit of what you think is your maximal effort, whether physical or mental, and keep on going. They are about training the mind to become comfortable with being uncomfortable – often very uncomfortable. These sessions are characterised by a feeling of dread beforehand, because you know that what you are intending to do is going to hurt – not to the point where you will be injured, but to the point where your body will hurt and be exhausted.

The red sessions, or honey badger sessions, are a mix of skill-based sessions and physical training. For example, the red box with a 1 inside it on a Monday afternoon represents a physical session. There is a large space after that – for recovery! Usually after a physical honey badger session, an athlete is exhausted and needs time to recover. The other two red sessions are slotted in amongst other things. These sessions are usually skill-based. For example, an athlete may choose to do a passing drill, or someone studying music may choose to do a chord drill (e.g. on the keyboard). The key to these sessions is to set them up to generate a 'boredom element'. For example, a basketball player's goal may be to shoot 300 jump shots before stopping that session. If their mind says, 'I am bored,' they simply remind it that they are the boss and it will finish the jump shots. Then they push on through the 'ceiling' and keep shooting.

Another idea is to set up one of your red sessions as an adversity session, during which you have a coach, a friend or a parent distract you while you practise (e.g. stand beside you talking, singing, saying funny jokes, etc). All the while, you still have to focus on your pre-performance routine and execution.

Over time, from doing these sessions, you will notice a development in mental fitness. You will find that you are able to push on during times of discomfort, when previously you would have given up. You will also be surprised at just how quickly the mind gets fit. It is no different from any other part of the body, so if you stop taking it to the mind gym, it will get unfit very quickly too.

HONEY BADGER MIND WEEK: EXERCISE 1

What are three Pathway 1 honey badger sessions you could do each week?

1. _____

2. _____

3. _____

2. The Intentional Failing Sessions

Fear of failing is incredibly powerful and something I see to some degree in most people I meet. Sure, some people have no fear of failing, embrace pressure with their whole being and unleash, but not many! Ironically, those who tell me they have no fear of failing seem to have it to the greatest degree, and hide it away. I have seen fear of failing destroy many careers by preventing athletes from fully 'unleashing and letting go'. The fear keeps them conservative when they should go for it; it keeps them careful when they should be instinctive – careful not to make mistakes, careful not to get it wrong, careful not to 'blow it' when winning and careful not to lose! Fear of failing is at the root of performance anxiety, which cripples some athletes to the point where they cannot eat or sleep properly leading up to a performance, and they vomit and/or visit the toilet many times before they perform. Fear of failing needs to be addressed in order for any athlete or other person to reach their potential, and that is what the intentional failing sessions have been designed for.

The importance of learning to fail in order to tap into your potential and play from a pure place is clearly evident in the following short passage from rugby player Brendon Leonard.

THE MENTAL FREEDOM FROM LEARNING TO FAIL!

When I became concerned with not making any mistakes, I would miss opportunities to attack. I became robotic! I had to train myself not to care. To do this you have to be prepared to fail at training 'intentionally' and be accepting of that. Embracing failing during the week, crazy as it sounds, then meant it did not weigh me down on game day. It freed me up to play my game! Learning to fail from a strong place is the key.

Brendon Leonard

'Harry' embracing the risk of failing fully and unleashing against the Highlanders at the Waikato Rugby Stadium in 2013.

The only way to overcome a fear is to embrace it. If you run away from something you fear, it will grow to consume you like a fire-breathing dragon! You must turn and face it. Essentially what I am saying is that a person must 'learn' how to fail and not care about failing before they will ever fully unleash. This does not mean that an athlete should become someone who wants to make mistakes, or does not strive to do things correctly. It merely means that they need to learn how to not have a deeply emotional reaction to failing. Unless they can achieve this, their mind will remain motivated not to fail, not to make mistakes and not to muck it up. The universe of 'not mucking it up' looks entirely different from the universe of striving to get it right!

Many coaches, parents, athletes and people in general struggle with the idea of having to learn how to fail before you can learn how to win. I have had many people tell me I am crazy or do not know what I am talking about when I introduce this concept. For example, here is a recent comment from a previous Olympic medallist (not a New Zealander) who brought his son along to talk to me about how I work.

> ### A PRETTY STRANGE IDEA!
>
> In all my years as an elite athlete, I never heard any coach or mind professional recommend such a thing [referring to the intentional failing sessions]. I have to admit, I am not sure what I think about that. I will give it some thought, but it seems a pretty strange idea to me!

Many people believe that fear of failing is critical to performing at your best. I couldn't disagree more. Fear of failing may help you hold to your weekly schedule and get you out of bed at 5 a.m. Fear of failing, however, is not as powerful as a deep love for your 'brothers' or 'sisters' in team sport, or a deep passion to get something perfect. Further, fear of failing is incredibly dangerous under the greatest pressure moments. The way a team or individual who fears failing deals with pressure is so different from those who do not. Fear at those times usually results in tension, freezing up or making uncharacteristic errors. The person who fears failing panics and is desperate for the event to finish.

When you do not fear failing, you are able to remain patient, composed and focused on your job, and do what needs to be done in pressure moments. At a pure level, pressure is not even experienced at all; these moments become something that an athlete cherishes and wants to absorb fully. When an athlete has no fear of failing, they actually want 'pressure moments' to last forever! That is what the intentional failing sessions will give you.

The intentional failing sessions are based on the fact that you cannot learn how to fail just by thinking about it. A person cannot overcome the fear of a barking dog by telling themselves they do not care about barking dogs, nor can they overcome a fear of upsetting people and being judged by others by telling themselves they do not care what others think. It is the same with fear of failing. You have to generate 'real' evidence – actual experiences in the world in which you live – that proves to your mind that you actually do not care. If you do not act in the way you want to live and the way you want your mind to be wired, when you try to convince your mind that you do not care, it will simply reply, 'Yes you do care! You care very much.' The intentional failing sessions generate the evidence to teach your mind that you do not care.

> **Warning**
> When you do your intentional failing sessions, it is critical that you never do anything that threatens your integrity as a person. That is, you never do anything that gives you, your family, your school, your team or your country a bad name. All I did was drive slowly in the fast lane, give a public speech and join a protest march. My behaviour did not compromise my values as a good person. I never did anything antisocial or illegal. I always live by my deep human values of care, compassion and integrity, no matter what intentional failing sessions I do. So must you when you do the sessions.

The good thing about the intentional failing sessions is that you do not have to do them very often to get great benefit from them. The key to making them really work, however, is to do them at times when your mind places great importance on what you are doing. For example, it is very easy to drop a ball on purpose when practising passing with your friends. However, it is a completely different thing to drop a ball on purpose in front of your coach! The golden rule with intentional failing sessions is that the payback or benefit you get from an exercise is directly related to the 'importance' of the context in which you do it. That is, when you make a mistake on purpose in a really important context, your mind thinks, 'They really are serious; they do not care about outcome!'

Intentional failing sessions are also incredibly beneficial for building deep self-acceptance. This comes from your learning that you do not actually care what others think, and do not need them to think good things about you for you to be a good person or to feel good. Self-acceptance grows best from experiences where you behave from courage, making intentional failing sessions perfect for this.

Further, intentional failing sessions are about providing opportunities where you practise 'letting go' and releasing into a GBM. You can only ever truly release if you do not care about failing. Over time, you will actually start to enjoy the intentional failing sessions because they will leave you feeling incredibly free and alive. They become a lot of fun! The letting go into the GBM comes so much easier from doing the intentional failing sessions because of the deepening self-acceptance.

There is another critical point to note when setting up your intentional failing sessions. **You cannot tell anyone what you are doing**. That is, you cannot drop the ball in front of the coach on purpose and then tell your friend that you did it as a mind gym exercise. If you do, it will take away all the 'power' of the exercise to grow your mind. Telling someone what you are doing will essentially make it a nothing event, and it will have no influence on your mind at all.

You can choose any context for an intentional failing session. For example, if you are having your weekly piano lesson, you can simply plan to muck up your piece at pre-determined places (e.g. you may plan to muck up your warm-up with your instructor, then the first rep of the third piece and the last bar of the last piece). If you play soccer and are having a skills-based session with the kicking coach, you can do the equivalent thing. If you were playing golf with the national selectors in a charity game, you could plan to three-putt the first hole and hit one ball OB on the 16th. If you are at school and want to overcome a fear of looking silly in front of your peers or getting things wrong in class, you could simply choose a lesson in which to ask a really silly question that everyone else will know the answer to. Make sure, though, that your simple question in class is not seen as being 'smart' or cheeky to the teacher. Maintain your integrity at all times!

The key, no matter what context you chose, is that no one knows what you are doing. When you fail and feel discomfort form in your tummy, simply roll these little phrases, or something like it, through your mind:

I don't care.

I don't care what they think.

You will find that the first few times your mind will care! It will care very much. It will likely scream at you, 'What are you doing!' That is when you can adjust what you say to yourself to help your mind understand what you are doing and why it is so critically important:

I will learn not to care!

I have to learn not to care if I am ever going to learn how to let go and achieve my potential!

HONEY BADGER MIND WEEK: EXERCISE 2

What are three contexts in which you could set up intentional failing sessions?

1. _____

2. _____

3. _____

Go and do them, then come back and write down a few thoughts about how they went, how it felt and how hard it was to get yourself to do them.

---

3. X Factor and Love of the Game

Perhaps one of the saddest things I see in my job is when someone pursuing greatness in a high-performance area loses the love of what they do. They start out loving their pursuit, but a high focus on outcome – especially negative outcome – and working on weaknesses while never feeling good enough, results in their love becoming 'polluted'. Eventually it just wears them down. And it is far more common than one might expect. I have so many examples of elite athletes coming to sessions not sure if what they are doing (i.e. full-time sport) is exactly what they want to do. They are lost and feel as though they fail far more than they ever succeed. They ask themselves, 'Do I really want to be doing this?' even if they are already among the best in the country, or the world. I imagine that some very good athletes have retired in the past because they have lost the spark, or the love for what they do. Adding X-factor or love-of-the-game sessions into your weekly schedule will keep the flame and love of what you do alive. You have to feed it!

Everybody, including every high-performance athlete, has an area that they excel in. I have yet to find someone who is terrible at everything! Even the youth I worked with in Auckland who were in the youth justice system had an X-factor area, or something that was their strength. Many were exceptional at music and art. Sadly, many were not very good at reading, maths and writing, and that had resulted in them feeling like failures at school. Hence they dropped out or found it easier to 'misbehave' than put up their hand and ask for help.

You will also have an X-factor area inside what you do, whether it is a certain area in a school subject, music or sport that you are pursuing. This will also likely be the reason you have chosen your particular pursuit. You would have heard the term 'X-factor' used a lot. It is often used by people to refer to something that someone is really good at. I see it as a specific part of what you do, not just what you do. For example, a basketball player may be very good at defence or three-point shots. A golf player may be good at putting or hitting from the sand. When athletes do these things, it fills them with confidence and pride; they feel alive when practising them. It feeds their soul! This is why practising in your X-factor area must be in your weekly schedule.

Unfortunately, the primary focus in modern-day sport is to try to 'fix' problems, and not grow strengths. As a result of this negative 'fix' approach, many athletes go days and weeks spending little time, if any, on their key strengths. This is what the X-factor sessions are about; you simply lock in times when you do what your strength is, for no other reason than the fun of it. The sessions are not about making your strength stronger, although that will occur, it is just for pure fun! Make sure you guard these times with your life. Nothing must prevent them from happening. If your mind asks you why you are doing a session, tell it:

Because I love it!

This is why I play this game [or the piano, etc]!

HONEY BADGER MIND WEEK: EXERCISE 3

What is your X-factor, or your greatest strength in what you do?

Write it here:

_____

_____

Now write down three things you could do in your X-factor area that would be great fun (e.g. hitting the driver for 30 minutes; hitting high-flying fades and long powerful draw hooks; playing your favourite song with your friends jamming in the shed)!

1. _____
2. _____
3. _____

Go and lock them in to your weekly schedule and tell your coach or parents or whoever you need to tell that these sessions are happening and why they are so important to your long-term happiness.

Now, go and have fun!

4. Patience Mind Gym

Perhaps the hardest thing for athletes, and people in general for that matter, I have noticed, is to be patient. Most are very impatient and expect things to be perfect today! Impatient people expect that they will reach their ultimate goal as soon as possible. For example, they might want to have made five million dollars by the time they are 25. When working on a skill or project, they want it achieved this week, and if not this week, then definitely this year. They are locked into the outcome – it is everything! They become desperate. Living in an impatient and desperate world, connected deeply to outcome, is very emotionally tiring. Usually, impatient people look forward to bedtime, as it is the only time they let themselves 'rest'.

Whenever I ask an athlete if they would like to be more patient, or if it would help them to be more patient, they always laugh, smile and reply 'Absolutely'! Most, however, have no idea how to grow patience, and feel that their impatience has control over them. They feel powerless to it. The impatience can be so powerful that they can never rest, struggling even to sit still for five minutes. They certainly have no relaxation or meditation sessions in their weekly schedule. They would not be able to stop for long enough to do them; they simply 'would not have the time'.

The ability to be patient is the biggest green flag for me that somebody has self-acceptance. When I see true patience in somebody, it is pretty exciting as a psychologist. True patience reflects a deep comfort, and acceptance of the self and one's mortality (accepting that one day you will die and that every project ends). It also means that a person is not connected to outcome and does not need outcome to feel OK. Essentially, someone with deep patience will have a mindset that they care more about how they do things (e.g. to be thorough in all they do) and less about the actual outcome itself. They will have reached a place where they will be accepting that they may or may not reach their dream, and are settled about either.

Obviously they want their dream, but they do not 'need' it. The difference between want and need is enormous. When an athlete wants a dream, but does not need it to make their life significant and worthwhile, they are able to achieve far deeper GBMs, and reach instinctual performance more consistently. Patient people end up living their dream rather than chasing it, and experience the very feelings others think they will get only from achieving their long-term goal. In that way, patience allows a person to live their dream before they even get there.

> **'ONE WHO IS IMPATIENT IN TRIVIAL MATTERS CAN SELDOM ACHIEVE SUCCESS IN MATTERS OF GREAT IMPORTANCE.'**
>
> CONFUCIUS

Earlier in this book I introduced the patience mind gym and listed various things you could do to help grow patience. Now you can place your patience mind gym onto your Honey Badger Mind Week. I think it is so important that you should do it every day! As I have already mentioned, mine is doing the dishes, and I do them for one and a half hours a day.

5. Relaxation and Imagery

The last element to be built into your Honey Badger Mind Week is your relaxation session. I have already spoken about the importance of relaxation. The great thing about relaxation is that you do not have to find the time to do it. Relaxation can be built in around other activities already on your schedule (e.g. you can do a relaxation session when taking a shower, doing your stretching or lying in bed in the morning). I like people to find a set time to do their relaxation, however, as this encourages patience and self-acceptance.

I also like people to build imagining into their relaxation sessions. I call this 'daydreaming with purpose'. They can mentally visualise MOPs of past performances and/or training and practice sessions, and look forward in time to rehearse various things they want to do in the future. Imagining while deeply relaxed allows the unconscious mind to be engaged, and it is in these moments that people say they unlock their true intuition. Pure intuition is very useful and allows people to come up with solutions for

Daydreaming with purpose: here is a picture of my eldest daughter 'daydreaming with purpose'. It was from finding her doing this one morning before school that I formed the phrase. She was sitting in one place staring into 'nowhere'. I asked her, 'What are you doing?' She replied, 'I am imagining my day.' I was amazed and asked, 'What do you mean?' She said, 'I have writing first thing this morning and I am imagining the story I am going to write, and we are playing forts at lunchtime so I was imagining the changes I want to make to our fort.'

problems that have been annoying them, or completely new ways of doing things. It is how most great evolutions in the way humans do things were conceived. Van Gogh said the lovely quote: 'First I dream my painting and then I paint my dream.'

Relaxation sessions and 'daydreaming with purpose' when athletes imagine performance become very special. Athletes often create a place in their house specially designed just for sitting or lying down and relaxing while imagining. Doing this becomes a 'success maker' or HOG for them – something they do across a week in order to be as prepared as they can be to perform.

A Real-Life Example of a Honey Badger Mind Week

I have included a real-life example of a Honey Badger Mind Week from a young athlete (Will) to give you an idea of what standard I expect from those talking about becoming world class. If you deeply want to become world class yourself, then this is the quality of mind week you should be aiming to create. You will have different exercises, but the attention to detail should be the same. Not only has Will evolved an excellent mind-training week, he is also reliable in following it. His weekly HOG stats record how many of his exercises he completes across the week.

> David,
>
> Just thought I'd email you and let you know the sort of things I did this week in regards to the Honey Badger Week, so I can get some feedback from you.
>
> Number 1 – living from philosophy: I was doing this either through some exercises at the gym or when running on the track. An example would be running 13 laps, and on the final lap, leaving nothing out there, crossing the line absolutely wasted.
>
> Number 2 – X-factor: I've been doing this throughout my week, by firstly doing lots of putting practice and then secondly trying to give myself that feeling when every time I pull it out of the bag and take the head cover off, I let myself know that this is my strong weapon! Working towards having this feeling every time I pull it out of the bag.
>
> Number 3 – patience: this has been a very good one lately. I've been using the cards! One time this week I actually took them to the course with me and when my mind and body wanted to quickly begin my practice by hitting balls and more balls, I got the cards out and took about 20 minutes going through them one at a time, saying to myself on every one, 'I will learn to be patient.' Secondly I tried to incorporate it into my driving – my actual

vehicle driving. Normally I am a driver who gets a little frustrated and I drive quite fast. This week I told myself I wasn't allowed to use the far left-hand lane, which is the lane for passing etc, and a few times I purposely put myself behind a car that was going very slowly. I had another good exercise tonight where I went to get an ice cream. I got to the door and it was packed! The line was almost out the door and just as my mind said to turn around and say bugger it, I said that this is a great opportunity for me, so I waited in line 30 minutes for an ice cream, hahahahaha! But great ice cream.

Number 4 – relaxation and bringing in the ninja monks: this one I've been usually doing lying down in bed. I try to feel that feeling when everything is going nicely out on the course and you're hitting it great, and then I also try to rehearse my greatest MOPs, which I have executed in the past.

The only bad and negative part of the week was my lack of intentionally failing. I'm sad to say it, but I need to admit it. I didn't do this once. I certainly did have a couple of opportunities to do it, and I passed on it! Silly me! Doesn't it just show how much I care about the wrong things! I know it's normal, but if I want to be the

> best I can be, I know this section is very crucial for me, and I am not going to let myself down this week. I'm going to do it when I can.
>
> Hope you and the family are well.
> Kind regards,
> Will

HONEY BADGER MIND WEEK: EXERCISE 4
Designing Your Own Honey Badger Mind Week

Your task is now to design your own Honey Badger Mind Week. You may choose to put all the key elements discussed in this section into your week, as they are all very important to 'unleashing your mind'. Or you may choose to be more selective about what you put on your schedule and include only those elements that will give you targeted benefit. If you are going to be selective, it is important that you reflect carefully on how your mind is 'wired'. If you fear failing, then intentional failing sessions will be critical. If you are an impatient person, then obviously a few patience mind gyms will be vital. Take your time deciding what exercises you will add, and where, when and how. For example, if you are doing a cardio honey badger red session, make sure you have plenty of time afterwards to recover!

PULLING YOUR WEEK TOGETHER AND BUILDING A POWERFUL PRE-PERFORMANCE MIND ROUTINE

I consider preparing to perform to be a week-long process, not something that just happens on the day of an event. Another reason for developing the mind week was to help athletes see that they can, and should, evolve their preparation across a period of time to get the best out of themselves under the pressure of performance. Living to your Honey Badger Mind Week will give you the additional benefit of training your mind to prepare immediately prior to performance. The strategies you use across the week can also be used when close to performing.

The diagram from the Honey Badger Mind Week included earlier will help explain this. If you look back at the diagram, you will see on the Saturday (game day) a gold box with a sequence of numbers going from four to one to KPI.

A rugby or soccer player may get to the ground one hour before the game, go into the changing room, sit down and take out the pack of cards that they use for their patience mind gym at home. This is the number four strategy on the diagram. They may say quietly to themselves while doing the card drill, 'Today I will be very patient,' and then imagine themselves being patient while playing out various situations they are expecting to occur.

If at any point people walk past while they are stacking their cards, and their mind feels embarrassed, they can say to themselves, 'And I do not care what anyone thinks of me.' Once they have finished their cards they can put them away quietly and get on with preparing physically for the game (e.g. get strapping from physio). The number three in their four, three, two, one sequence is the drill where they do whatever it is they deeply love in their sport. A fullback in either sport may just love kicking the ball or attacking, so will do those exercises first when starting their skill-based warm-up for the game, thereby injecting excitement, passion and fun.

Number two on the list is intentional failing. A great example of how this could be built into the preparation routine would be a goal kicker in rugby missing his first kicks on purpose, without telling anybody, when doing his warm-up kicks. You can guarantee that if there is a crowd they will be watching, and if the coach(es) are out they will be observing the kickers too. The goal kicker can simply say to himself inside his head, 'I don't care,' and because he has being practising intentional failing for weeks, his mind knows what he is doing and why. The mind settles, the unconscious is allowed to come forward and the player drops into instinctive mode.

Finally, number one on the list is the drill or activity that unleashes the Pathway 1 philosophy. In rugby, the honey badger is popular, so many players really get stuck in to the final physical warm-up drill, usually a defensive tackling drill, to unleash the physical aggression required to play a combat sport. Given the intensity of the number one drill, it is vital to do this as close to the start of the game as possible, otherwise you risk getting too 'amped up' too early!

The Key Performance Instinct part of the sequence is sitting quietly within two or so minutes of running out onto the park (e.g. in rugby or soccer) or court (in squash or tennis) and accessing your KPI or feeling. This is when you take your mind to the GBM you have been imagining during the week and including in training and practice sessions. Usually accessing the KPI or GBM comes easiest when an athlete is physically quite warm, so the last drills you do are critical in order to 'fire' pure body-mind connection. The last thing I like athletes to do before they perform (e.g. in rugby or soccer it could be just as the referee looks at their watch immediately prior to signalling the start of the game) is to imagine their very first job in vivid detail. It is by applying high intent to your very first act that you will tip into instinct.

In summary, I will reiterate what I started this chapter with. The Honey Badger Mind Week is perhaps the most important thing out of everything I do with the people I work with. It is through this you can gain long-term benefits from the work you have done establishing key areas such as your Pathway 1 philosophy. Sure, all the other elements are critical for establishing the foundation of the week, but the actual training of the key parts from the book is what makes the difference.

Most people have read personal development or performance psychology books before. Usually, though, most people return to 'old habits' a short time after reading the books! The Honey Badger Mind Week is perhaps a key difference in this book that will ensure you have long-term follow-on benefits from the material covered. The Honey Badger Mind Week is not just an exercise, it is the structure to making your mind training a Habit of Greatness.

We all have a choice, every day, and every action we make: a choice to be great, average or poor at what we do. The Honey Badger Mind Week is a way to help you train your mind so that when you act, and when you make a choice, you choose to be great from habit. You will find that initially it may be quite difficult to get your mind to commit fully to the Honey Badger Mind Week exercises. This is no big deal; it simply reflects that your mind is not yet fully fit! Do not be hard on yourself for not being 100 per cent on your weekly exercises or drills; simply remind yourself that it is called a mind gym for a reason, and that it will get stronger and stronger as a habit over time. You will eventually find that your mind and soul will feed off doing the exercises. That is why they become habit. They will become a very important part of your week, and eventually this will result in you 'unleashing your mind'!

FINAL MIND WARRANT OF FITNESS CHECK

Well done, you have made it to the end of the book! I hope you have had just as much fun working through it as I had writing it. By getting this far, you have already joined a very special group of people – most people do not complete self-improvement books! The stats regarding this are remarkable. Only 10 per cent of people finish self-improvement books. That means 90 per cent of people never finish them! This statistic highlights just how important discipline and perseverance are to long-term success. Now you can see why I spend one-and-a-half-hours a day doing my dishes! It has taken me from the group of people who never finish a thing into the group who do. Your finishing means that you are now in the top 10 per cent – something to be proud about.

In addition to finishing the job off, attention to detail in what you do is critical for reaching potential. The following section gives you a way to reflect on how thorough you have been in completing the exercises. Each of the key elements covered in the book are summarised, along with a **red**, **yellow**, **green** rating system for you to use.

Remember, each element covered in the book is a building block of the entire foundation to your life and pursuit, no matter what that is (i.e. sport, music, business, school, etc). If you have only partially completed an area then it will eventually compromise your potential. If you have substandard and/or incomplete areas, go back and do them again.

Rate yourself out of 10 first, with 10/10 being perfect. Then ask your parent(s), partner, mentor or coach to rate you in each area as well. There are double scales for each key point, so you can sit down with at least one key person to review how you are tracking. Sometimes we can fool ourselves that we are doing better or worse than we actually are. Getting feedback from someone you trust and know will be honest with you is worth its weight in gold!

> **Rating Guide**
>
> **0** = not completed (i.e. you have lived in the **red** box)
>
> **5** = completed but just gone through the motions
> (i.e. lived in the **yellow** box)
>
> **10** = absolutely nailed it in a world-class way
> (i.e. lived in the **green** box)

You should now be living your Pathway 1 philosophy of courage.

You should now have a very clear and precise philosophy for life and whatever you are pursuing. For example: 'I would rather fail from a strong place than ever succeed from a weak one!' 'Courage!' 'No wasted minutes!' 'Who dares wins!' 'Be the LION!' 'Live!' You should have shared it with the key support people around you and they should be able to now see it reflected in everything you do.

Your rating:
0 ----------------------------------5----------------------------------10

Parent, partner or coach rating:
0 ----------------------------------5----------------------------------10

General comments about this area:

_____
_____
_____
_____
_____

Your Impossible Dream should be clear and written down somewhere.
You should have shared your dream with your inner circle (i.e. parent(s), coach, etc) and evolved the way you talk with others about it, using 'I will' language whenever anyone asks you about your long-term goals (e.g. media, other members at your club, etc).

Your rating:
0 ----------------------------------5----------------------------------10

Parent, partner or coach rating:
0 ----------------------------------5----------------------------------10

General comments about this area:

_____
_____
_____
_____
_____

You should now have committed fully to your Impossible Dream.
You should have connected with a world-class mentor, built your Green Box (daily habits directly linked to success) and be 'paying the price' required each day to eventually 'earn' the dream.

Your rating:
0 ----------------------------------5----------------------------------10

Parent, partner or coach rating:
0 ----------------------------------5----------------------------------10

General comments about this area:

_____
_____
_____
_____
_____

You should have developed your strategic plan to success.
Your plan should start at the end point (e.g. world number one in whatever you do) and have incredibly high detail about what this looks like (e.g. videos, pictures, stats, etc). The plan should then step back from there to now. You should have a lot of detail about how good each key element needs to be to reach the dream, and an objective measure of how good you are right now in each of those areas. You should have a lot of detail for the coming year and what its targets are (e.g. stats such as greens in regulation in golf, strength and power in the gym, etc) and how you intend to achieve these. You should also have a lot of detail for what you will do each week and each day. (Note: make sure you have time-off planned as well!) Your plan should look as though you are living by the philosophy 'No wasted minutes!'

Lastly you should have presented your strategic plan to your support people, and everyone should have agreed on whose job is what, how often the plan will be reviewed and how you will know progress is being made. It sounds like a lot, and it is, but get it done and watch your growth explode!

Your rating:
0 ----------------------------------5----------------------------------10

Parent, partner or coach rating:
0 ----------------------------------5----------------------------------10

General comments about this area:

_____
_____
_____
_____

You should have built powerful non-outcome success rules and be clear on what is most important.
You should now be really clear that living with non-outcome expectations or success rules is very important to achieving long-term potential. You should be living with helpful, powerful non-outcome success rules in all you do. You should have shared both your old unhelpful and new helpful success rules with your key support people on your 'committee'. Everyone should be clear about what success really is and have agreed on what will be discussed when reviewing your performance with you and each other.

Your rating:
0 ----------------------------------5----------------------------------10

Parent, partner or coach rating:
0 ----------------------------------5----------------------------------10

General comments about this area:

_____
_____
_____
_____
_____

You should now understand MOP universe and be living deeply with this mindset.
This should involve having educated your key support people about MOP and MOS universes. You should have formed your key performance language questions. Whenever anyone asks you how something has gone, people around you should hear your key performance language coming out in your answers, regardless of the results. You should be keeping a MOP book for training and practice as well as performance.

Your rating:
0 ----------------------------------5----------------------------------10
Parent, partner or coach rating
0 ----------------------------------5----------------------------------10

General comments about this area:

_____
_____
_____
_____

You should be training the Goose Bump Moment.
You should have trialled using your Pathway 1 philosophy, relaxation techniques (hooo hummm; sitting still, thinking nothing; one, two) and imagery to find the best way to access deep instinct immediately before performing. You should be starting to feel as though you are 'letting go' and just dropping into your performance as you get better and better at this. Your pre-performance routine should be repeatable, and others should see you going through the same stages before you perform every time, no matter how 'important' the event.

Your rating:
0 ---------------------------------5---------------------------------10
Parent, partner or coach rating:
0 ---------------------------------5---------------------------------10

General comments about this area:

You should now be doing 'deep practice'.
Your practice sessions should be based on objective evidence and plans. That is, anything you do should be directly related to the stats and the areas that have been identified as key for the next block of work, whether that is the next week, month or six months. Everything you do must be planned! You should be breaking practice into technical sessions and instinct sessions. Technical sessions will be highly thought-based and conscious-mind anchored. Instinct sessions will be when you practise 'letting

go' and performing from your philosophy – therefore from instinct – without thoughts polluting the space. You will be learning through MOPs and working hard to ignore every MOS altogether. As already mentioned, you should be keeping a MOP book at practice.

Your rating:
0 --------------------------------5--------------------------------10

Parent, partner or coach rating:
0 --------------------------------5--------------------------------10

General comments about this area:
_____
_____
_____
_____
_____

You should have built your Honey Badger Mind Week.
You should now realise how important it is to train your mind to be mentally fit, and how it will not just happen by itself. You will now have your mind gym exercises slotted throughout your normal week's schedule. You will either be doing all the strategies introduced in 'The Honey Badger Mind Week' chapter, or have selected ones that work for you. If the latter is the case, then it is critical that those you have selected suit how your mind works. For example, if you are an impatient person, it is critical that you have daily patience mind gyms. If you fear failing or being judged, it is vital that you have intentional failing sessions. (Remember that you cannot let anyone know you are doing failing sessions.) You will have established a pre-performance routine (refer to the 4, 3, 2, 1 box for Saturday in the Honey Badger Mind Week diagram) that is

based on the same mind drills or exercises you are doing across the week to assist you to get into the best mindset before you perform.

Your rating:
0 ----------------------------------5----------------------------------10

Parent, partner or coach rating:
0 ----------------------------------5----------------------------------10

General comments about this area:

_____
_____
_____
_____
_____

CLOSING NOTE

There are many 'shoulds' in the summary above. I make no apologies for that. If you are truly committed to finding out how good you can get at your pursuit, these things are very important. They have to happen. They have to happen for you to evolve and train your mind to the level required to allow your physical and instinctual potential to unleash.

Lastly, thank you. Thank you for grabbing this book and taking the plunge into instinct. I wish you and those close to you the very best Pathway 1 success.

MOP UNIVERSE!
DG

AFTERWORD

Nothing you go on to achieve in your sport or pursuit, or life in general for that matter, will be worth anything unless you live a great life, and are a great guardian of our children and environment. After all, that is what life is really about. It is about being a good person – a loving friend and family member, and a loving parent if you choose to have children. It is about looking after the planet in order to pass it on to the next generation in a better state than when it was passed to you.

That is why I finish with this small note about the 'Pacific garbage patch', a phenomenon introduced to me midway through 2013. I had never heard of it. I watched the following clip before going to bed, and could not sleep. It was like a nightmare come true. Note that this clip is dated early 2000. It has been almost 15 years since it was made. That means another 15 years of human garbage or waste has poured into the Pacific since it was filmed.

www.youtube.com/watch?v=M7K-nq0xkWY

Since watching this video, I have done my best to be a better guardian of the Earth. We are working incredibly hard at home to be zero plastic and use only recyclable tin, steel and glass. It is a great myth that most plastic is recycled; most plastic (and I mean most) ends up either in landfills or goes down drains into small streams, then rivers, before passing out into the seas and oceans around the world. This is perhaps the greatest risk to human existence of our time, as scientific research is showing that plastic toxicity is now in our oceans' food chain. Fish eat the plastic as it breaks down into various sizes, then fish eat fish, and we eventually eat the fish. The long-term health effects on humans and our entire eco-systems become quite monumental!

Please, consider going plastic-free and tell others about it as well. We have the technology for biodegradable plastics; however, companies would not make as much profit, and that is why they do not use more of it. Be part of the solution, not the problem!

APPENDIX

PERFORMANCE LANGUAGE FOR YOU, YOUR PARTNER, PARENTS AND COACHES TO USE WITH EACH OTHER

The lists below suggest questions you can use when reviewing your practice, training and performance (i.e. as soon as the final 'whistle' goes), and at any other time you think about or talk about your pursuit (e.g. in the car, bus or plane). The first four questions are highlighted because I consider them the most powerful. I would encourage you to trial them as part of deciding which ones you will use.

At first you will have to force yourself and those around you to think and speak like this, as unfortunately this is not how most people are wired to think. You may even have to write your questions or thoughts down. Over time, though, it will become more automatic. The more people you can get to use this language with you (e.g. coaches, parents, friends) the faster it will become a habit.

List 1: To Build Confidence and Self-Belief
- **What am I most proud of about the way I performed, trained or practised today?**
- **What was one thing I learnt today that will help me fine-tune my training for tomorrow/this week and help me WIN next time?**
- **What is one piece of evidence from today that proves I can achieve my dream?**
- **How was I successful today? (Review your core expectations to answer this one.)**
- What was one thing I learnt today that I am now really looking forward to applying next time I practise, train or perform?
- What did I most enjoy today?
- What am I now really looking forward to next time I practise, train or perform?
- What was the most exciting thing from today's practice, training or performance?
- What was one way that I did not give up and/or believed in myself today?
- What is one example of when I showed strong killer instinct?
- What will be my best memory from today?
- What was one thing from today that proves my plan is working?
- What is one thing from today I can work on mastering that in the future will really give me the edge over all other competitors?

List 2: To Savour Victory and Moments of Excellence and Perfection
This list will help teach your mind to accept that you are as good as you are, and you have no idea just how much potential you have or how good you can become!
- What was one thing from today's practice, training or performance that proves I can achieve my sporting dream?
- What was the best thing about my performance today?
- What was one thing I nailed perfectly today?
- What was one thing from today that shows I am a very skilled or excellent athlete?

- What great or excellent part of today's performance am I most proud of?
- What was my favourite part of the performance today?
- What was one thing from today's performance I really enjoyed?
- What is one thing from today's performance I am really looking forward to trying to replicate next week?
- What was the most exciting part of this performance, practice or training?
- When was one time I nailed killer instinct and finished the job off?
- When was one time my mental game was perfect, strong or sound?

Come up with a list of three or four questions that best fit you.

Write down some mock answers to help get your mind used to using performance language, then use this language all the time, with as many people as possible.

Make sure you have selected the best questions for you.

Do this by rating how your questions/answers make you feel out of 10 for:

a. confidence and self-belief that you can achieve your dream   /10
b. enthusiasm to practise, train or compete/perform again   /10

Ratings should be high! (8–10/10)

Partners, friends and family – when using these questions please do not let your athlete:

a. make any excuses (e.g. blame the ref, travel, etc)
b. use 'give-up' talk (e.g. 'I will never be as good as . . . ' or 'We will never beat them!')
c. seek reassurance from you that they are actually good enough. Instead, if they come home grumpy, for example, go over and give them a cuddle and say, 'Don't worry; there is another game next week' or 'You will be OK', etc)

d. talk negatively or throw a tantrum, etc. If they do, simply say, 'When you are ready to talk/review, just let me know.' Then go and have a coffee, give them some space and only engage when they start using their performance language questions or similar strong and courageous language and self-talk.

Do support them to be courageous and get back to work, stick to their plan towards their dream, and commit everything and expect nothing in return. Reward this with praise and encouragement.

ACKNOWLEDGMENTS

I want to thank all the people who have supported me in various ways over many years . . . without you I would not be where I am today . . . the depth of my gratitude cannot be represented in words . . . there are just too many of you to print your names here . . . that is how 'lucky' I have been . . . you know who you are.

I also want to thank the athletes who allowed me the privilege of being part of their journeys. You are exceptional people. I have learnt so much from you. Thank you too, to those of you who pressured me to write about Pathway 1 so others could have access to it, without your request to do this the book would not have been started!

Even then, finishing the book almost did not happen. At the end when the book was complete, my finger hovered over the delete button with a serious intent of wiping five years' work, as writing the book was so counter to my core values of humility and anonymity. It was your stories within the book and our shared vision of inspiring other New Zealanders to live their DREAMs that spurred me on to submit it to the publisher and finish the job off!

ABOUT THE AUTHOR

David Galbraith is a New Zealand registered clinical psychologist. He began specialising in sport and business in 2006 and he now works full time with elite athletes and teams from various sports. He has been the Chiefs Super Rugby Team sports psychologist for the last seven campaigns, and is also working with the All Blacks Rugby 7s team, the NZ Women's Sevens team, the NZ BMX team, NZ Women's Football team and NZ Golf. He worked with the Magic netball team during 2012 and 2013 and is working with a number of individual elite olympic athletes.

IMAGE CREDITS

Page 6	Stephen Donald, *Kevin Booth sportpix*
Page 16	Lisa Carrington, *Getty Images*
Page 19	Jay Carter and Mark Brown, *Jamie Troughton*
Page 25	Matt Cameron, *Matt Cameron*
Page 26	Edmund Hillary and Tenzing, © Royal Geographical Society (with IBG)
Page 27	Mark Brown, *Mark Brown*
Page 29	Golf course, *David Galbraith*
Page 33	Hana Seifert, *Hana Seifert*
Page 35	Brendon Leonard, *Kevin Booth sportpix*
Page 42	Laura Langman, *Laura Langman*
Page 44	Luke Toomey, *Luke Toomey*
Page 45	Sarah Cowley, *Sarah Cowley*
Page 53	Will Monery, *Will Monery*
Page 58	Sarah Cowley, *Sarah Cowley*
Page 66	Laura Langman, *Laura Langman*
Page 68	Brad Kendall, *Brad Kendall*
Page 79	Lake Karapiro, *David Galbraith*
Page 85	Chiefs, *Getty Images*
Page 86	Richard and Stephen, *Kevin Booth sportpix*
Page 94	Bricks, *David Galbraith*
Page 95	Dishes, *David Galbraith*
Page 101	Fence, *Reon Sayer*
Page 107	Matt Perry, *Matt Perry*
Page 116	Dean Eggers, *Dean Eggers*
Page 131	Lisa Carrington, *Getty Images*
Page 141	My eldest daughter, *David Galbraith*
Page 145	Joelle King, *Joelle King*
Page 153	My daughters, *David Galbraith*
Page 163	Magic, *Noeline Taurua*
Page 173	Sarah Walker, *Daniel Franks*
Page 176	Richard Kahui, *Kevin Booth sportpix*
Page 179	Grace fishing, *David Galbraith*
Page 188	My daughters, *David Galbraith*
Page 192	Dave Feeny, *Dave Feeny*
Page 208	Hana Seifert, *Hana Seifert*
Page 219	Luke Toomey, *Luke Toomey*
Page 230	Mark Brown, *Dean Eggers*
Page 251	Brendon Leonard, *Kevin Booth sportpix*
Page 261	My eldest daughter, *David Galbraith*
Page 263	Will Monery, *Will Monery*

Published by David Galbraith
Contact David Galbraith at mopuniverse@gmail.com

Copyright © David Galbraith, 2015

The right of David Galbraith to be identified as the author of this work in terms of section 96 of the Copyright Act 1994 is hereby asserted.

Designed by Mary Egan
Cover designed by Anna Egan-Reid
Produced by Mary Egan Publishing
www.maryegan.co.nz

Printed in China

All rights reserved. Without limiting the rights under copyright reserved above, no part of this publication may be reproduced, stored in or introduced into a retrieval system, or transmitted, in any form or by any means (electronic, mechanical, photocopying, recording or otherwise), without the prior written permission of both the copyright owner and the above publisher of this book.

ISBN 978-0-473-30932-9